TEST YOUR BRIDGE TECHNIQUE

# DEFENDING
# SUIT CONTRACTS

D1008186

*David Bird*

*Tim Bourke*

MASTER POINT PRESS • TORONTO

**Master Point Press**
331 Douglas Ave.
Toronto, Ontario, Canada
M5M 1H2
(416) 781-0351
Website:        http://www.masterpointpress.com
Email:          info@masterpointpress.com


**Library and Archives Canada Cataloguing in Publication**

Bird, David, 1946-
        Defending suit contracts / David Bird & Tim Bourke.

(Test your bridge technique)
ISBN 1-894154-80-0

1. Contract bridge--Defensive play.  I. Bourke, Tim
II. Title.  III. Series: Bird, David, 1946-  Test your bridge technique.

GV1282.42.B568 2005          795.41'53          C2004-906794-X

| | |
|---|---|
| Editor | Ray Lee |
| Cover and interior design | Olena S. Sullivan/New Mediatrix |
| Interior format | Luise Lee |
| Copy editing | Suzanne Hocking |

Printed in Canada by Webcom Ltd.

1 2 3 4 5 6 7          09 08 07 06 05

# PLANNING THE DEFENSE AGAINST A SUIT CONTRACT

Were you hoping to buy a book that would show you how easy defense can be? Sorry about that! Even impecunious bridge writers, hoping to promote their books, cannot pretend that there is a set of magic formulae to guide you to the winning defense. Of course there are some excellent general guidelines, taught to beginners. When you are past that stage you have to do two things: you must count and you must think. You count to gather evidence, and you must think in order to determine the best chance of defeating the contract. (This will be the aim throughout this book. Imagine that you are defending at IMPs or rubber bridge, rather than trying to save an overtrick in a matchpoint pairs event.)

Let's look at counting first. What do you count? This is the list:

**High-card points**. If declarer has indicated his point-count range during the auction (by bidding, or passing), you keep a count on the points he shows and deduce what remaining cards he might hold.

**Shape**. As soon as possible, you attempt to gain a 'count of the hand'. This means discovering how many cards each player holds in a suit. The more you play bridge, the more you will appreciate how important this is.

**Tricks**. You count how many certain tricks declarer has, also how many the defenders have. For example, if you can count three certain tricks for the defenders, you will need two more to beat 3NT.

It's time for a hand. Let's look at a typical defense that many players would get wrong. It's not difficult if you are prepared to count.

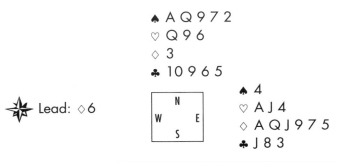

♠ A Q 9 7 2
♡ Q 9 6
◇ 3
♣ 10 9 6 5

Lead: ◇6

```
      N
  W       E
      S
```

♠ 4
♡ A J 4
◇ A Q J 9 7 5
♣ J 8 3

| WEST | NORTH | EAST | SOUTH |
|------|-------|------|-------|
|      |       |      | 1NT   |
| pass | 2♡*   | 3◇   | 3♠    |
| pass | 4♠    | all pass |    |

South opens a 15-17 point 1NT and reaches 4♠ after a transfer sequence. West leads the ◇6 and you win with the ◇A, declarer following with the ◇4. What is your plan for the defense?

Let's count points first. Dummy holds 8 points, you have 13 and declarer has 15-17. How many points does this leave for your partner? To make the total up to 40 he will hold between 2 and 4 points. If he holds the ◇K the situation is hopeless for the defense, so assume that declarer holds that card.

Now let's count tricks. You can see two tricks with your minor-suit aces and will therefore need two more tricks to beat the game. What chances can you see of achieving this aim?

One possibility is to find partner with the ♡K. When he holds this card, a switch to the ♡4 is likely to give you three heart tricks — enough to beat the contract.

Suppose next that declarer holds the ♡K. What will the defensive prospects be if you switch to a club at Trick 2? Since you cannot score more that one trick in hearts (declarer can discard one of dummy's hearts on his ◇K), you will need two club tricks to beat the contract. For this to be possible, West must hold at least ♣K-Q-x. By counting points, as we did above, you know that West cannot hold more than 4 points!

So, the correct defense is to switch to a low heart. It is the only real chance of breaking the contract. If declarer turns up with the ♡K you can be fairly sure that the contract was unbeatable.

Before we talk about counting shape we need to discuss how you should signal in defense. It is fairly standard across the bridge-playing world to signal 'count' when declarer plays a suit. A high spot card shows an even number of cards in the suit and a low spot card shows an odd number. Suppose declarer is playing in 4♠ and has this diamond suit:

◇ K Q J 8 3

◇ 9 7 2          ◇ A 10 4

◇ 6 5

Declarer leads a diamond towards dummy and West follows with the ◇2 to show that he has an odd number of diamonds. Placing West with three diamonds and declarer with two, East may decide to hold up the ace for one round. When dummy has no entry in another suit, this will restrict declarer to one diamond trick.

This is an alternative lie of the suit:

◇ K Q J 8 3

◇ 9 7          ◇ A 10 4

◇ 6 5 2

Now West plays the ◇9 on the first round. It is a useful understanding to have with your partner that from four cards you will signal with the second-best card followed by the fourth-best. Note that in practice you can nearly always tell from the bidding or from the lengths displayed in the other suits whether partner holds four cards or two. On that basis West's ◇9 cannot be from a four-card holding and suggests a doubleton. East will hold up both on the first round and the second round. Declarer will then score only two diamond tricks rather than four.

Such signaling is common practice and we move now to a more interesting, and perhaps controversial, area. How should you signal when your partner leads a suit and you do not need to attempt to win the trick by playing high in third seat? Many players use 'attitude signals' in such a situation — a high card to encourage a continuation and a low card to discourage. This can be useful in some situations. In others there is advantage to be gained by using count signals. Many experts around the world do indeed prefer to use count signals.

Suppose you lead the ♡3 against 4♠ and this is the lie of the suit:

$$♡ \; Q \, J \, 6$$

$$♡ \; K \, 10 \, 8 \, 3 \qquad\qquad ♡ \; 9 \, 7 \, 4 \, 2$$

$$♡ \; A \, 5$$

Not one of your brightest efforts and dummy's ♡Q wins the trick. Do you need partner to give you the ♡2, to tell you that you have made an unfortunate lead? No! You know that already. You would much prefer that he told you something useful — his count in the suit. In this case he would play the ♡7 (second best from four) and you would be part way towards building up a complete count of the hand. Not only that, if you were stuck for an exit card later in the play, you would be grateful to know that declarer's ♡A was now bare and you could safely play a heart.

Count signals can also assist you when you need to cash the setting tricks against a contract. Suppose you are West here:

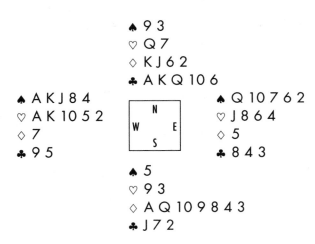

♠ 9 3
♡ Q 7
◊ K J 6 2
♣ A K Q 10 6

♠ A K J 8 4          ♠ Q 10 7 6 2
♡ A K 10 5 2         ♡ J 8 6 4
◊ 7                  ◊ 5
♣ 9 5                ♣ 8 4 3

♠ 5
♡ 9 3
◊ A Q 10 9 8 4 3
♣ J 7 2

| WEST | NORTH | EAST | SOUTH |
|------|-------|------|-------|
|      |       |      | 3◇    |
| 4◇*  | 5◇    | pass | pass  |
| dbl  | all pass |   |       |

Your 4◇ bid showed a two-suiter in the majors. You lead the ♠K and partner plays the ♠2, declarer following with the ♠7. What now? If you are playing count signals, you know that partner has an odd number of spades. It is dangerous to play the ♠K next because declarer might ruff, draw trumps and run the club suit. At Trick 2 you lead the ♡K and partner signals with the ♡8. He is showing an even number of hearts. Counting around the table, you therefore know that declarer has one remaining heart and that a second top heart played from your hand will escape unruffed. You continue with the ♡A and beat the contract.

Here is another deal where a count signal from partner will guide you to the correct defense:

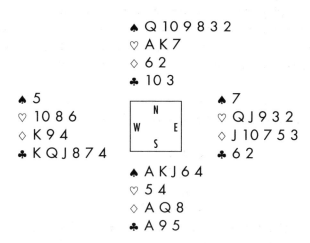

```
              ♠ Q 10 9 8 3 2
              ♡ A K 7
              ◇ 6 2
              ♣ 10 3
♠ 5                            ♠ 7
♡ 10 8 6          N            ♡ Q J 9 3 2
◇ K 9 4      W         E       ◇ J 10 7 5 3
♣ K Q J 8 7 4     S            ♣ 6 2
              ♠ A K J 6 4
              ♡ 5 4
              ◇ A Q 8
              ♣ A 9 5
```

You lead the ♣K against 6♠. Declarer wins with the ♣A, draws trumps and eliminates the hearts (by playing the ace and king and ruffing the third round). He then plays the ♣9 to your jack. What will you do next?

If declarer began with ♣A-9 doubleton, a club return will give him a ruff-and-sluff (he will be able to throw a diamond from dummy and ruff in his hand, easily making the contract). Your only option is to play a diamond, hoping that East holds the ◇Q. If instead declarer began with ♣A-9-5, you can safely play the ♣Q now and live to score a trick with your ◇K. Which is it to be?

There is no guess if you play count signals. When the cards lie as in the diagram, East will have played the ♣6 followed by the ♣2. You will then be able to place him with two clubs, leaving declarer with three cards in the suit. You will therefore exit with the ♣Q and beat the game.

When East started with ♣6-5-2 he would play the ♣2 on the first round and follow with a higher card. Knowing that declarer had indeed started with only two clubs, you would exit in diamonds. This would beat the contract when East held the ◇Q. As in many situations you are spared a guess if you play count signals. If you play attitude signals, you have to guess.

We have looked at the potential benefits of count signals. No doubt you currently play attitude signals when partner leads to a suit. When do you think this type of signal is most useful? One situation is where you have led from A-K-x-x and would like partner to encourage if has the queen or a doubleton. Another is when you have led from Q-J-9-x and dummy wins with the ace. You would like partner to tell you if he holds the king.

Attitude signals are indisputably strong opposite an ace or queen lead. Some players reckon that count signals work best opposite a king lead. Hoping to get the best of both worlds, they play a method of opening leads known as: 'ace (or queen) for attitude, king for count'. In other words when they lead an ace or a queen to a trick partner is expected to give an attitude signal. When they lead a king they want partner to give a count signal.

How does this method work? Suppose you are on lead against 4♡ and hold ◇A-K-5-2. You lead the ◇A because you want partner to encourage or discourage the lead. If instead you were on lead against a five- or six-level contract, you would lead the ◇K because it would be more important for you to know how many rounds would stand up.

There are advantages and disadvantages in every signaling method and it is not our intention to persuade you one way or the other.

Nevertheless, we will have to put this book on a firm foundation by using a fixed method of signaling throughout. We will assume that the defenders are using attitude signals when partner leads a suit, except when a king is led. In that case they will signal count. It is for you to decide, at the end of the book, if you were impressed by the method. Signaling will not be relevant on most of the problems anyway. The emphasis will be on thinking logically and counting.

We will assume the use of 'count discards' also. Using this scheme, you discard from the suit that you can best afford, usually one that you do not want partner to lead. At the same time, you show your count in this suit. A discard of the ♡8, for example, indicates lack of interest in hearts and an even number of cards in that suit.[1]

Well, all too soon we have reached the end of our introductory section. Count, think, signal to help your partner, and stay awake! What could be easier than defending perfectly? Unfortunately, almost everything...

1. There are many different discarding methods and we recognize this one may not be to your preference. However, we had to pick something!

# Problem 1

 Lead: ♣Q

♠ Q J 6 4
♡ A Q J 3
◇ 6 5
♣ 9 5 2

♠ K 10 5 3
♡ 9 6
◇ A 7
♣ A 8 7 6 3

| WEST | NORTH | EAST | SOUTH |
|------|-------|------|-------|
|      |       |      | 1◇ |
| pass | 1♡ | pass | 3◇ |
| pass | 3♠ | pass | 5◇ |
| all pass | | | |

West, your partner, leads the ♣Q. You win with the ace and the king falls from South. How will you continue?

# Problem 2

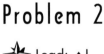 Lead: ♠J

♠ K Q 5 2
♡ J 9 6
◇ 10 5
♣ A K Q 8

♠ 10 9 8 7 3
♡ A 8
◇ A 8 3
♣ J 9 2

| WEST | NORTH | EAST | SOUTH |
|------|-------|------|-------|
|      | 1NT | pass | 4♡ |
| all pass | | | |

Your partner leads the ♠J, won by dummy's ♠K. Three top clubs come next, South following once and then throwing the ◇9 and the ◇J. He then leads a low trump from dummy. How will you defend?

# Problem 3

Lead: ♠9

```
                    ♠ K 10 4
                    ♡ 9 8 3
                    ◇ K J 2
                    ♣ K J 5 3
```

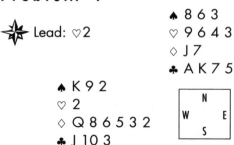

```
                              ♠ A Q J 5 3 2
                              ♡ J 2
                              ◇ A 10 6
                              ♣ 8 6
```

| WEST | NORTH | EAST | SOUTH |
|------|-------|------|-------|
|      |       | 1♠   | 2♡    |
| pass | 2♠*   | pass | 4♡    |
| all pass |   |      |       |

West leads the ♠9 (he would lead the middle card from 9-x-x). The ♠10 is played from dummy and you win with the ♠J. What now?

# Problem 4

Lead: ♡2

```
                    ♠ 8 6 3
                    ♡ 9 6 4 3
                    ◇ J 7
                    ♣ A K 7 5
```

```
♠ K 9 2
♡ 2                    N
◇ Q 8 6 5 3 2      W       E
♣ J 10 3               S
```

| WEST | NORTH | EAST | SOUTH |
|------|-------|------|-------|
|      |       | 2♡*  | dbl   |
| pass | 3♣*   | pass | 3♠    |
| pass | 4♠    | all pass |   |

North's 3♣ shows around 8-10 points. You lead the ♡2 to partner's king. He continues with the ♡A, dropping South's ♡Q, and then plays the ♡J. South ruffs with the ♠Q. What is your plan for the defense?

♠ Q J 6 4
♡ A Q J 3
◇ 6 5
♣ 9 5 2

♠ 9 7
♡ 10 8 7 4 2
◇ 8 3
♣ Q J 10 4

♠ K 10 5 3
♡ 9 6
◇ A 7
♣ A 8 7 6 3

♠ A 8 2
♡ K 5
◇ K Q J 10 9 4 2
♣ K

| WEST | NORTH | EAST | SOUTH |
|------|-------|------|-------|
|  |  |  | 1◇ |
| pass | 1♡ | pass | 3◇ |
| pass | 3♠ | pass | 5◇ |
| all pass |  |  |  |

*3NT would have been hopeless and North-South bid well to reach 5◇ instead. You are sitting East and your partner leads the ♣Q. You win with the ace and the king falls from declarer. What next?*

South, who made a jump rebid, is almost certain to hold the 16 points that are missing outside the club suit. Even if he holds only six diamonds, you can count five diamond tricks, two spade tricks with the finesse, and four heart tricks — a total of eleven. Your best hope is to cut declarer off from the dummy, which can be done if he holds only two hearts. At Trick 2, you return a heart, won with the king. When the king of trumps is led, you win immediately (so that you still have a trump left) and return your remaining heart, which declarer must win in the dummy. Deprived of four heart tricks, declarer will now lead the spade queen. Should you cover or not?

If you do cover, declarer will simply win with the ♠A, draw trumps and return to dummy with the ♠J to enjoy the remaining heart winners. Play low and declarer will have no way to make the contract. He will doubtless try his luck with a third round of hearts, which you will ruff.

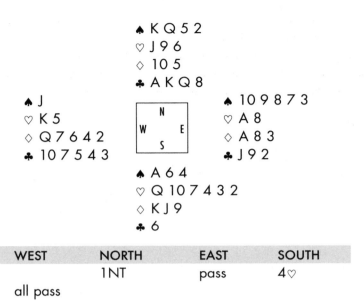

| WEST | NORTH | EAST | SOUTH |
|------|-------|------|-------|
|      | 1NT   | pass | 4♡    |
| all pass |    |      |       |

*With no particular reason to place the contract in the North hand, South spurns a transfer response and leaps directly to 4♡. Sitting East, you see your partner lead the ♠J. This is almost certain to be a singleton, since you can see the ♠10-9 in your hand and a doubleton jack is one of the worst leads in the game. Declarer wins with dummy's king and cashes three clubs, following once and then discarding the nine and jack of diamonds. He then leads a low trump from dummy. How will you defend?*

When the deal arose in an international match between France and Belgium, both East players made the same mistake. They rose with the trump ace to give their partner a spade ruff. West ruffed all right but the ruff was with the king and the defenders scored only three tricks, allowing the game to make.

As East, you should count the tricks available to the defense. You will score the trump ace, a spade ruff and (you hope) the ◇A. How can you score a fourth trick? You cannot hope to give partner two spade ruffs, after rising with the ♡A. South surely has a six-card trump suit for his bid and that leaves West with only two trumps. The contract can be beaten only if your partner can win the first trump and cross in diamonds for a spade ruff. You should therefore play low on the first trump. Another benefit from defending in this way is that declarer may finesse into partner's ♡Q-x.

(Declarer could have made the contract by playing a fourth round of clubs, throwing his last diamond. This would have broken the link between the defenders and allowed him to make the game.)

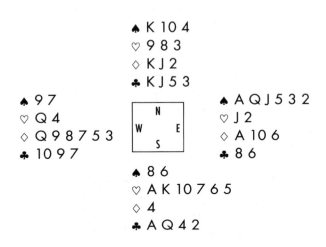

| WEST | NORTH | EAST | SOUTH |
|------|-------|------|-------|
|      |       | 1♠   | 2♡    |
| pass | 2♠*   | pass | 4♡    |
| all pass |    |      |       |

*West, your partner, leads the ♠9 against South's heart game. The ♠10 is played from dummy and you win with the ♠J. What now?*

Partner's ♠9 lead is either a singleton or a doubleton. (Few players lead 'top of nothing' from such as 9-8-7 nowadays. They prefer to lead either the second-best or the bottom card.) You continue with the ♠A and both the closed hands follow suit. Your ◇A is likely to score a third trick for the defense. What is the best chance of a fourth trick?

If partner holds the singleton ♡Q or ♡Q-x or ♡10-x-x, a third round of spades will promote a trump trick for the defense. Should you therefore lead a spade at Trick 3? No, because if declarer holds only one diamond he will be able to discard it. Even if you do promote a trump trick, the contract will still be made. So, to guard against declarer holding a singleton diamond you should cash the ◇A at Trick 3. Only then do you lead a third round of spades. When the cards lie as in the diagram, your partner has a magic ♡Q-x and you beat the contract.

Suppose next that the dummy was a little weaker, with a diamond holding of Q-J-2. There would then be a dual purpose in cashing the ◇ A. If partner held the ◇ K and a trump holding that offered no chance of a promotion, he could encourage a diamond continuation by playing a high card.

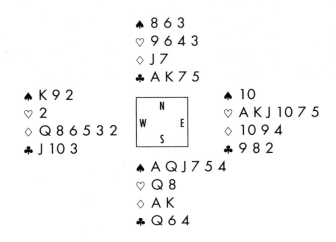

|       | WEST  | NORTH   | EAST     | SOUTH |
|-------|-------|---------|----------|-------|
|       |       |         | 2♡ *     | dbl   |
|       | pass  | 3♣ *    | pass     | 3♠    |
|       | pass  | 4♠      | all pass |       |

*North's 3♣ promised around 8-10 points. With a weaker hand he would have responded with an artificial 2NT (Lebensohl). Sitting West, you lead the ♡2 and your partner wins with the ♡K. He continues with the ♡A, dropping South's ♡Q and then plays the ♡J. South ruffs with the ♠Q. What is your plan for the remainder of the defense?*

Partner has shown up with eight points in hearts, so that does not leave any room for a big defensive card elsewhere. By far the best chance of beating the contract is to score two trump tricks. Your ♠K is worth a trick anyway, so you should think carefully before using the card for an overruff. By conserving all three trumps, you may find that you can make a trick with the ♠9 as well as the ♠K.

Instead of overruffing, you should discard a diamond. Because your partner holds the ♠10 the contract is now doomed. Whether or not declarer finesses the ♠J on the first round of trumps, you will make two trump tricks.

Look what happens if you mistakenly overruff the ♠Q with the ♠K. Declarer will win your return and draw the outstanding trumps with the ace and jack, making the game. The potential of scoring two trump tricks would have been easier to see if you held K-10-x in the trump suit. K-9-x is just as valuable, of course, when partner holds the ♠10.

# Problem 5

Lead: ♠A

♠ 8 7
♡ 10 4
♢ K 8 6
♣ K J 9 8 7 2

♠ A 5
♡ J 6
♢ A J 5 4 2
♣ 10 6 5 3

| WEST | NORTH | EAST | SOUTH |
|------|-------|------|-------|
|      |       | 2♠*  | 4♡    |

all pass

Sitting West, you lead the ♠A against South's game in hearts. Partner follows with an encouraging ♠9. How will you plan the defense?

# Problem 6

Lead: ♡K

♠ 8 5 2
♡ 8 4 2
♢ A Q J
♣ A Q J 5

♠ A 9
♡ A 7
♢ 9 8 6 4 2
♣ 7 6 3 2

| WEST | NORTH | EAST | SOUTH |
|------|-------|------|-------|
| 2♡*  | pass  | pass | 2♠    |
| pass | 4♠    | all pass |    |

You are sitting East and your partner leads the ♡K against South's spade game. What is your plan to defeat the contract?

# Problem 7

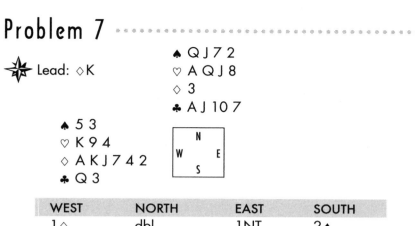

Lead: ◇K

|  | ♠ Q J 7 2 |
|  | ♡ A Q J 8 |
|  | ◇ 3 |
|  | ♣ A J 10 7 |

♠ 5 3
♡ K 9 4
◇ A K J 7 4 2
♣ Q 3

| WEST | NORTH | EAST | SOUTH |
|------|-------|------|-------|
| 1◇ | dbl | 1NT | 2♠ |
| pass | 4♠ | all pass | |

Sitting West, you lead the ◇K against South's spade game. Partner follows with the ◇5 and South plays the ◇6. How will you continue the defense?

# Problem 8

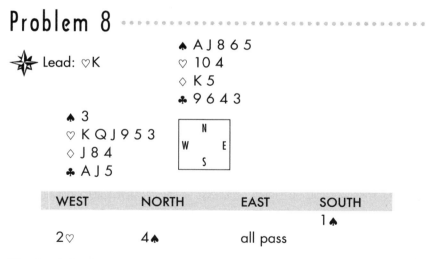

Lead: ♡K

|  | ♠ A J 8 6 5 |
|  | ♡ 10 4 |
|  | ◇ K 5 |
|  | ♣ 9 6 4 3 |

♠ 3
♡ K Q J 9 5 3
◇ J 8 4
♣ A J 5

| WEST | NORTH | EAST | SOUTH |
|------|-------|------|-------|
|  |  |  | 1♠ |
| 2♡ | 4♠ | all pass | |

You lead the ♡K, partner playing the ♡2. Declarer wins with the ♡A and plays the ♠K, followed by the ace and king of diamonds. He then plays the ♡10 to your jack (♡6 from partner). What will you do next?

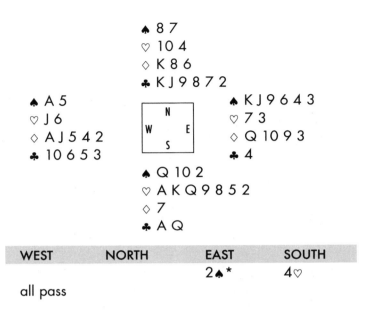

♠ 8 7
♡ 10 4
◇ K 8 6
♣ K J 9 8 7 2

♠ A 5
♡ J 6
◇ A J 5 4 2
♣ 10 6 5 3

♠ K J 9 6 4 3
♡ 7 3
◇ Q 10 9 3
♣ 4

♠ Q 10 2
♡ A K Q 9 8 5 2
◇ 7
♣ A Q

| WEST | NORTH | EAST | SOUTH |
|------|-------|------|-------|
|      |       | 2♠*  | 4♡    |

all pass

*Sitting West, you lead the ♠A against South's game in hearts. Partner signals with an encouraging ♠9. How will you plan the defense?*

The original West lost no time in continuing with a second spade which East won with the ace. East could now have beaten the contract by playing a third round of spades for his partner to ruff with the ♡J in front of dummy's ♡10. The diamond ace would then be the setting trick. Unfortunately this was not obvious to East. He decided to switch to his singleton club, hoping that West could win and give him a club ruff. Not the best move! Declarer won with the ♣A, drew trumps and claimed an overtrick.

West was quick to blame his partner but in fact he could have made life much easier for poor East. Did you spot how to do this? At Trick 2 you should cash the ◇A before playing a second spade. It would then be obvious to East that declarer holds the ♣A. When partner wins the second round of spades there will be no temptation to switch to a club. He will play a third round of spades, hoping to find you with a trump higher than dummy's 10, and be satisfied to see you produce the ♡J.

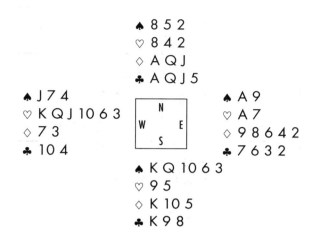

♠ 8 5 2
♡ 8 4 2
◇ A Q J
♣ A Q J 5

♠ J 7 4
♡ K Q J 10 6 3
◇ 7 3
♣ 10 4

♠ A 9
♡ A 7
◇ 9 8 6 4 2
♣ 7 6 3 2

♠ K Q 10 6 3
♡ 9 5
◇ K 10 5
♣ K 9 8

| WEST | NORTH | EAST | SOUTH |
|------|-------|------|-------|
| 2♡ * | pass | pass | 2♠ |
| pass | 4♠ | all pass | |

*You are sitting East and partner leads the ♡K against four spades. What plan do you have to beat the spade game?*

You can expect two heart tricks and a further trick from the ace of trumps. Declarer has the minor suits locked up, even if your partner does hold one of the kings there. You must therefore hope for a second trick from the trump suit. Overtake the king of hearts with the ace and return your remaining heart. Your partner will win with the ♡10 and continue with the ♡Q. What now?

If you defend passively, discarding on this trick, declarer will make the contract. He will ruff low in the South hand, cross to dummy with a diamond and lead a trump. You cannot do any damage if you rise with the ace, so you will play low. Declarer's king will win the trick and he will return to dummy for a second trump lead. Your ace will appear, sparing him any guess, and declarer will be home free.

What if you ruff the third round of hearts with the ♠9? That's no good either. Declarer will overruff with the ♠10 and again pick up the trumps for just one loser. The only winning move is to ruff with the ♠A. Your partner's ♠J-x-x will move one rung higher on the ladder and will now score the setting trick. Similarly, if partner had held ♠Q-x, you would ensure the defeat of the contract.

Does any other point occur to you? Since your partner held a potentially promotable ♠J, it would have been more helpful for him to lead a low heart on the third round. This would have made it clear that he wanted you to ruff the trick.

Leading a low card when you want partner to ruff is an important technique. Here is another deal where it would show to advantage:

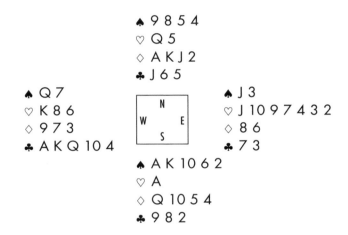

```
                    ♠ 9 8 5 4
                    ♡ Q 5
                    ◇ A K J 2
                    ♣ J 6 5
  ♠ Q 7                              ♠ J 3
  ♡ K 8 6              N             ♡ J 10 9 7 4 3 2
  ◇ 9 7 3          W       E         ◇ 8 6
  ♣ A K Q 10 4         S             ♣ 7 3
                    ♠ A K 10 6 2
                    ♡ A
                    ◇ Q 10 5 4
                    ♣ 9 8 2
```

| WEST | NORTH | EAST | SOUTH |
|------|-------|------|-------|
|      |       |      | 1♠ |
| 2♣ | 3♣* | pass | 4♠ |
| all pass | | | |

Your partner overcalls 2♣ and subsequently leads the ♣K against South's spade game. You play the ♣7 on the first round and the ♣3 when West continues with the ♣A. What should you do when West plays the ♣Q at Trick 3?

If partner holds six clubs you would like to ruff with the ♠J, hoping to knock a hole in declarer's trumps and promote a trick for partner (a play known as an 'uppercut'). If, instead, West has only five clubs you would prefer to discard and then ruff with the ♠J on a fourth round of clubs. How can you tell?

Only West knows how many clubs he holds! It is his duty to lead a low card when he wants you to ruff. When he leads the ♣Q on the third round, he is telling you that three clubs will stand up and you should discard on that trick.

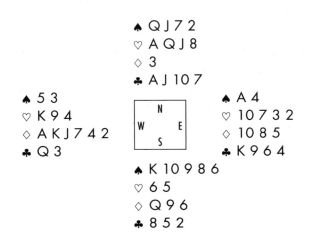

♠ Q J 7 2
♡ A Q J 8
◇ 3
♣ A J 10 7

♠ 5 3
♡ K 9 4
◇ A K J 7 4 2
♣ Q 3

♠ A 4
♡ 10 7 3 2
◇ 10 8 5
♣ K 9 6 4

♠ K 10 9 8 6
♡ 6 5
◇ Q 9 6
♣ 8 5 2

| WEST | NORTH | EAST | SOUTH |
|------|-------|------|-------|
| 1◇ | dbl | 1NT | 2♠ |
| pass | 4♠ | all pass | |

*Sitting West, you lead the ◇K against South's spade game. Partner follows with the ◇5 and South plays the ◇6. How will you continue the defense?*

Your ♡K is not looking too healthy under dummy's ♡A-Q-J, so it looks as if you will score only one trick in the red suits. The only realistic chance of beating the spade game is to find partner with both the ♠A and the ♣K. In that case you may be able to score one club trick, one trump trick and a ruff, giving you four tricks in all.

At Trick 2 you should switch to the ♣Q. Declarer wins with dummy's ♣A and leads a trump from dummy. Your partner will rise with the ♠A, cash the ♣K and give you a club ruff. That's down one.

Suppose you were watching this deal in some expert tournament. You can be sure that every West would switch to the ♣Q after very little thought. Now transport the deal to an average game at the club. The results might well be quite different. Those West players who act on general principles rather than making a plan might view a club switch as 'too dangerous' and switch to a trump instead. You can avoid such a trap by trying to picture partner's hand. He has shown some points with his 1NT bid and there is an excellent chance that he will hold the two black honors that you need to defeat the contract.

As a final point, what signal do you think East should give on the first trick. When there are no further tricks to be taken in the suit led (in this case because dummy holds a singleton), it makes good sense for East to give a suit preference signal. East's $\diamond$ 5, his lowest card in the suit, should suggest a club switch.

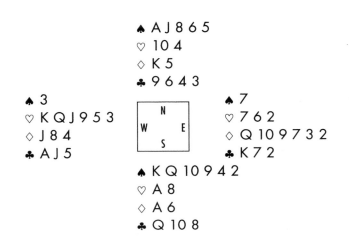

| WEST | NORTH | EAST | SOUTH |
|------|-------|------|-------|
|      |       |      | 1♠    |
| 2♡   | 4♠    | all pass |   |

*Sitting West, you lead the king of hearts against South's game in spades. Partner plays the ♡2 and declarer wins with the ♡A. After drawing one round of trumps with his king, declarer plays the ace and king of diamonds and throws you on lead with the ♡10. What will you do next?*

There is no pressing need to cash any tricks, so you should exit safely if you can. If declarer has a heart left, it will be safe for you to play a third round of hearts. Does declarer have a heart left? No, and you know this because partner gave you a count signal of the ♡2 at Trick 1. He therefore started with three hearts to declarer's two.

How about a third round of diamonds? Is that safe? Again partner will have given you a count signal in the suit — showing an odd number of cards. However, you do not need a signal to read the diamond position. If declarer had another diamond he would have ruffed it before throwing you on lead!

So, declarer's shape must be 6-2-2-3. A ruff and discard will allow him to throw a club from his hand and make the contract, so you will have to play a club. You need partner to hold the ♣K and therefore you exit with a low club. On this occasion partner does hold the required card. He wins with the ♣K and returns a club, putting the contract down one.

# Problem 9

 Lead: ♣10

```
              ♠ J 8 7 3
              ♡ 5 2
              ◇ A Q J 6 4
              ♣ J 4
                          ♠ K 9 4
         ┌─────────┐      ♡ 8 7 4
         │    N    │      ◇ K 9 2
         │ W     E │      ♣ Q 7 6 2
         │    S    │
         └─────────┘
```

| WEST | NORTH | EAST | SOUTH |
|------|-------|------|-------|
|      |       |      | 2♣ |
| pass | 3◇ | pass | 4NT |
| pass | 5♣* | pass | 6♡ |
| all pass | | | |

Your partner leads the ♣10. Declarer wins with the ace and plays the ◇5 to West's ◇8 and dummy's ◇Q. How will you defend?

# Problem 10

 Lead: ♠Q

```
              ♠ K 8
              ♡ J 7 6 3 2
              ◇ K 9 7 2
              ♣ K 7
  ♠ Q J 10 2
  ♡ Q 9 5
  ◇ Q 10 5
  ♣ 10 6 4
```

| WEST | NORTH | EAST | SOUTH |
|------|-------|------|-------|
|      |       |      | 1♡ |
| pass | 4♡ | pass | 6♡ |
| all pass | | | |

South wins your ♠Q lead with the ace and plays the ♡A, East discarding a club. After cashing the ♡K, the ♣A-K and dummy's ♠K, he plays a trump to your queen. What now?

# Problem 11

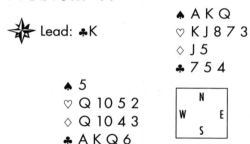

Lead: ♣K

♠ A K Q
♡ K J 8 7 3
◇ J 5
♣ 7 5 4

♠ 5
♡ Q 10 5 2
◇ Q 10 4 3
♣ A K Q 6

| WEST | NORTH | EAST | SOUTH |
|------|-------|------|-------|
|      |       |      | 1♠    |
| dbl  | rdbl  | pass | pass  |
| 2♣   | 3♣    | pass | 3♠    |
| pass | 4♠    | all pass |    |

Sitting West, you lead the ♣K. Partner plays the ♣2 (count) and you play two more top clubs, everyone following. What next?

# Problem 12

Lead: ♣3

♠ 5 3
♡ A K
◇ K 7 6 3 2
♣ A Q 6 2

♠ 10 8 4
♡ Q 10 8 7 5 4
◇ Q 10 5
♣ 9

| WEST | NORTH | EAST | SOUTH |
|------|-------|------|-------|
|      |       |      | 1♣    |
| 1♠   | 2◇    | pass | 3◇    |
| pass | 5♣    | all pass |    |

Declarer wins the trump lead in his hand and plays a second trump to the ace. How will you defend, sitting East, when he then leads the ◇2?

```
                    ♠ J 8 7 3
                    ♡ 5 2
                    ◇ A Q J 6 4
                    ♣ J 4
   ♠ Q 10 5         ┌─────────┐      ♠ K 9 4
   ♡ 6             │    N    │       ♡ 8 7 4
   ◇ 10 8 7 3      │ W     E │       ◇ K 9 2
   ♣ 10 9 8 5 3    │    S    │       ♣ Q 7 6 2
                   └─────────┘
                    ♠ A 6 2
                    ♡ A K Q J 10 9 3
                    ◇ 5
                    ♣ A K
```

| WEST | NORTH | EAST | SOUTH |
|------|-------|------|-------|
|      |       |      | 2♣ |
| pass | 3◇ | pass | 4NT |
| pass | 5♣* | pass | 6♡ |
| all pass | | | |

*South heads for a slam as soon as he hears a positive response. Sitting East, you see your partner lead the ♣10. Declarer wins with the ace and immediately plays the ◇5 to West's ◇8 and dummy's ◇Q. How will you defend?*

When declarer holds two diamonds, it is good defense to hold up the king. Declarer will then score at most two diamond tricks — possibly only one if he decides to repeat the diamond finesse. Here, though, your partner plays the ◇8 on the first round. This is a count signal that shows an even number of diamonds. If West has a doubleton diamond, a hold-up will make no difference. A more dangerous situation is that West's ◇8 is a second-best card from 10-8-7-3. In that case it could be disastrous to hold up the ◇K. After pocketing one diamond trick, declarer will continue with the ◇A and discard one of his spade losers. He can then claim the contract.

So, when your partner shows an even number of cards in the suit, you should win the first round of diamonds. On this deal declarer will be left with two further losers in spades. Suppose instead that West were to show an odd number of diamonds (three, leaving South with two). You would then hold up the ◊ K in the hope that declarer had only eleven tricks available.

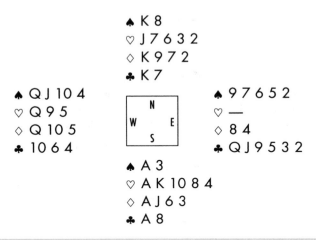

♠ K 8
♡ J 7 6 3 2
◇ K 9 7 2
♣ K 7

♠ Q J 10 4
♡ Q 9 5
◇ Q 10 5
♣ 10 6 4

♠ 9 7 6 5 2
♡ —
◇ 8 4
♣ Q J 9 5 3 2

♠ A 3
♡ A K 10 8 4
◇ A J 6 3
♣ A 8

| WEST | NORTH | EAST | SOUTH |
|------|-------|------|-------|
|      |       |      | 1♡    |
| pass | 4♡    | pass | 6♡    |
| all pass |   |      |       |

*You lead the ♠Q and declarer wins with the ♠A. He continues with the ace of trumps, not looking at all pleased when East shows out, discarding a club. He draws a second round of trumps with the king and cashes the ♠K, followed by the ace and king of clubs. His next move is to throw you in with the trump queen. What should you do next?*

You don't need partner's count signals to tell you that declarer has no further cards in the black suits. Had he held a third club or spade, he would have ruffed it in the dummy before throwing you in. So, if you return either black suit you will give declarer a ruff-and-sluff.

Carrying his calculations no further, the original West exited with the ◇5 in the hope that his partner would produce the ◇J. Alas, it was South who produced this card and the slam was made.

A count of the hand would have told West that declarer's shape was 2-5-4-2. It follows that a ruff-and-sluff will not assist him. Declarer is welcome to throw a diamond from one hand or the other; he will still be left with a loser in the suit. If West exits in either black suit, instead of making the first play in diamonds, the slam will go down one.

```
                    ♠ A K Q
                    ♡ K J 8 7 3
                    ◇ J 5
                    ♣ 7 5 4
    ♠ 5                              ♠ J 8 3
    ♡ Q 10 5 2         N            ♡ 9 6 4
    ◇ Q 10 4 3    W        E        ◇ 9 7 6 2
    ♣ A K Q 6         S            ♣ 9 3 2
                    ♠ 10 9 7 6 4 2
                    ♡ A
                    ◇ A K 8
                    ♣ J 10 8
```

| WEST | NORTH | EAST | SOUTH |
|------|-------|------|-------|
|      |       |      | 1♠ |
| dbl | rdbl | pass | pass |
| 2♣ | 3♣ | pass | 3♠ |
| pass | 4♠ | all pass | |

*Sitting West, you lead the ♣K. This asks for a count signal and your partner contributes the ♣2. You continue with two more high clubs, all following. Three tricks are in the bag. How will you continue?*

Dummy has 14 points and you have 13. That leaves only 13 points between declarer and your partner. It is a near certainty that declarer holds the three missing big cards — the heart ace and the diamond ace-king. In that case, how can the defenders possibly score a fourth trick?

Unlikely as it may be, you must hope that your partner holds ♠J-x-x. A fourth round of clubs will then beat the contract. If declarer chooses to ruff with one of dummy's honors, partner's ♠J will be promoted. If instead declarer discards from dummy, planning to ruff in his hand, your partner will ruff with the ♠J.

It's not usually a good idea to give a ruff-and-sluff, of course. Here you are able to read declarer's hand with some accuracy and can be almost certain that no more tricks will come your way in the side suits.

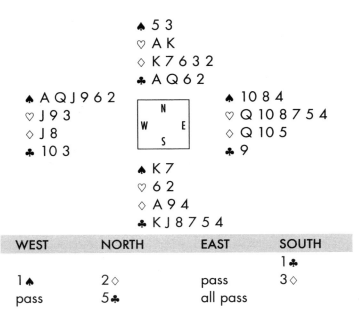

♠ 5 3
♡ A K
◊ K 7 6 3 2
♣ A Q 6 2

♠ A Q J 9 6 2
♡ J 9 3
◊ J 8
♣ 10 3

♠ 10 8 4
♡ Q 10 8 7 5 4
◊ Q 10 5
♣ 9

♠ K 7
♡ 6 2
◊ A 9 4
♣ K J 8 7 5 4

| WEST | NORTH | EAST | SOUTH |
|------|-------|------|-------|
|      |       |      | 1♣    |
| 1♠   | 2◊    | pass | 3◊    |
| pass | 5♣    | all pass |   |

*You are sitting East and partner leads the ♣3. Declarer wins in the South hand and crosses to dummy with the ♣A. How will you defend when he then leads the ◊2?*

You're unimpressed with the bidding, we realize, and all the players at your club would easily bid the cold game in notrumps; however, this is a book on defense not bidding. Your opponents will often arrive in the wrong contract and it will then be up to you to beat it!

So what diamond do you play at Trick 3? If you carelessly follow with the ◊5, declarer will 'duck into the safe hand'. He will cover with the ◊9, allowing your partner to win with the ◊J. West cannot attack spades effectively from his side of the table and the contract will be made. Indeed, if West fails to cash his ♠A immediately, declarer will discard both his spade losers and score an overtrick.

To prevent South from ducking the first round of diamonds into the safe hand, you must play high in the second seat. On the layout we show, it will be good enough to insert the ◊10, forcing South's ◊A. If declarer persists with diamonds, you will win the third round with the

◇Q and kill the game with a spade switch. Rising with the ◇10 will not be good enough, however, when South holds four diamonds and your partner has a singleton ◇J.

The very best defense is to rise with the ◇Q on the first round. When partner started with a singleton ◇J, this will fall under South's ◇A. Your ◇10 will then win the third round of the suit as before and kill the contract. When the cards lie as in the diagram, however, your partner must be sure to drop the ◇J under declarer's ace to avoid having to win the second round of the suit!

Let's suppose that you do play a high diamond in the second seat and declarer is forced to win with the ace. If he reads the diamond position he may decide to switch horses, refusing to play a third round of the suit. He may play dummy's two top hearts instead, leaving this position:

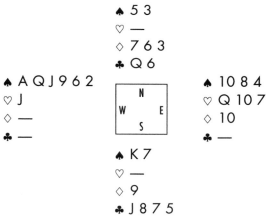

♠ 5 3
♡ —
◇ 7 6 3
♣ Q 6

♠ A Q J 9 6 2
♡ J
◇ —
♣ —

♠ 10 8 4
♡ Q 10 7
◇ 10
♣ —

♠ K 7
♡ —
◇ 9
♣ J 8 7 5

When declarer leads the ♠3 from dummy, it is no time for you to be asleep in the East seat. If you follow with the ♠4, declarer will cover with the ♠7, won by your partner. Once again declarer will have achieved his objective of ducking into the safe hand. Your partner can cash the ♠A next but he will then have to give a ruff-and-sluff, allowing the contract to make.

To beat the contract you must insert the ♠8. If declarer follows with the ♠7, partner will also play low and you will be able to cash your diamond winner. If instead your ♠8 is covered by the king and ace, your partner must be brave and return a low spade to your ten, so that you can cash the winning diamond.

# Problem 13

Lead: ◇7

```
            ♠ Q 8 3 2
            ♡ J 6 3
            ◇ J 4
            ♣ A J 9 7
                        ♠ K 6
         N              ♡ 2
      W     E           ◇ A K Q 10 9 5
         S              ♣ 10 8 6 5
```

| WEST | NORTH | EAST | SOUTH |
|------|-------|------|-------|
|      |       | 1◇   | 3♡    |
| 3♠   | 4♡    | pass | pass  |
| dbl  | all pass |   |       |

West leads the ◇7 to your ◇Q. You play the ◇A and West plays the ◇6. You cash the ♠K successfully at Trick 3. How will you continue?

# Problem 14

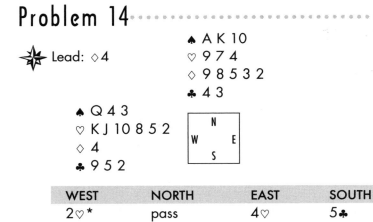Lead: ◇4

```
            ♠ A K 10
            ♡ 9 7 4
            ◇ 9 8 5 3 2
            ♣ 4 3
  ♠ Q 4 3
  ♡ K J 10 8 5 2      N
  ◇ 4               W   E
  ♣ 9 5 2             S
```

| WEST  | NORTH | EAST | SOUTH |
|-------|-------|------|-------|
| 2♡*   | pass  | 4♡   | 5♣    |
| all pass |    |      |       |

Sitting West, you lead the ◇4 against five clubs. East wins with the ◇A and declarer follows with the ◇J. When your partner returns the ◇6, South plays the ◇Q and you ruff. What will you do next?

# Problem 15

 Lead: ◇6

          ♠ K 10 8
          ♡ J 2
          ◇ Q J 4
          ♣ A 8 6 5 2

♠ 5 4 3
♡ K 10 7 6 5
◇ 6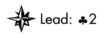
♣ J 10 9 4

| WEST | NORTH | EAST | SOUTH |
|------|-------|------|-------|
|      |       | 1◇   | 1♠    |
| pass | 2◇*   | pass | 3♠    |
| pass | 4♠    | all pass |   |

You lead the ◇6 against 4♠. Partner wins with the ◇K, cashes the ◇A and leads the ◇2, declarer playing the ◇3, the ◇7, and the ◇9. How will you defend from this point?

# Problem 16

 Lead: ♣2

          ♠ Q 6 5 2
          ♡ K J
          ◇ 9 7 4 2
          ♣ A 7 4

                    ♠ 9 7
          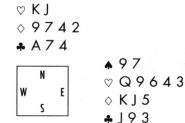   ♡ Q 9 6 4 3
                    ◇ K J 5
                    ♣ J 9 3

| WEST | NORTH | EAST | SOUTH |
|------|-------|------|-------|
|      |       |      | 1♠    |
| pass | 3♠    | pass | 6♠    |
| all pass |   |      |       |

Declarer wins with dummy's ♣A and leads the ◇2. What card will you play to this trick? What is your general plan for the defense?

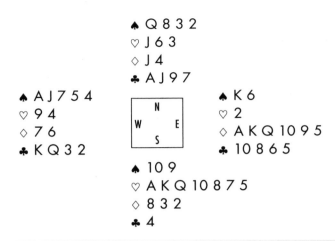

♠ Q 8 3 2
♡ J 6 3
◊ J 4
♣ A J 9 7

♠ A J 7 5 4
♡ 9 4
◊ 7 6
♣ K Q 3 2

♠ K 6
♡ 2
◊ A K Q 10 9 5
♣ 10 8 6 5

♠ 10 9
♡ A K Q 10 8 7 5
◊ 8 3 2
♣ 4

| WEST | NORTH | EAST | SOUTH |
|------|-------|------|-------|
|      |       | 1◊   | 3♡    |
| 3♠   | 4♡    | pass | pass  |
| dbl  | all pass |   |       |

*West leads the ◊7 and, sitting East, you win with the ◊Q. When you cash the ◊A, partner follows with the ◊6 (showing a doubleton). You cash the ♠K successfully at Trick 3. How should you continue?*

If your partner holds only five spades for his 3♠ bid, the setting trick will come from his ♠A. If instead he holds six spades, the only realistic chance of beating the contract is to play a third diamond. This will promote a trump trick for partner when he holds ♡Q-x (or, conceivably, a singleton ♡K). Which of these lines of defense offers the best chance?

There is no need to guess! Your partner should give a count signal when you lead the ♠K. Here he will play the ♠4. Since this is the lowest spot-card out, you will know that he holds five spades rather than six. You return a spade and beat the contract. If instead West had held ♠A-J-9-7-5-4, he would play the ♠9, to show six spades. You would then return a diamond, playing for a trump promotion.

Even if your normal signaling method is 'attitude', it would be pointless here. You know that West holds the ♠A when your ♠K wins. He knows that you know, too! So, West should give a count signal anyway.

When this deal was originally played in an international trial, a top-class professional pair allowed the game to make. West played an 'encouraging' ♠7. East read it as a count signal and switched back to diamonds! Declarer ruffed in the dummy, drew trumps and ran his remaining trumps. This was the end position:

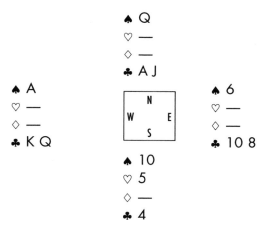

When the last trump was played, West had to surrender one of his black-suit guards. 'Thank you, partner!'

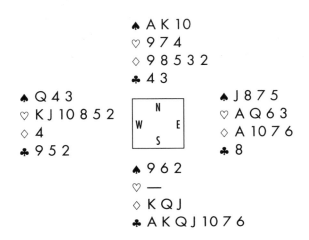

♠ A K 10
♡ 9 7 4
◇ 9 8 5 3 2
♣ 4 3

♠ Q 4 3
♡ K J 10 8 5 2
◇ 4
♣ 9 5 2

♠ J 8 7 5
♡ A Q 6 3
◇ A 10 7 6
♣ 8

♠ 9 6 2
♡ —
◇ K Q J
♣ A K Q J 10 7 6

| WEST | NORTH | EAST | SOUTH |
|------|-------|------|-------|
| 2♡ * | pass | 4♡ | 5♣ |
| all pass | | | |

*Sitting West, you lead your singleton diamond against 5♣. East wins with the ◇A and declarer follows with the ◇J. When your partner returns the ◇6, South plays the ◇Q and you ruff. What will you do next?*

When the deal arose, West gave the matter insufficient thought and returned a heart at Trick 3. Declarer ruffed and drew trumps in three rounds. He then unblocked the ◇K and crossed to dummy with a top spade. It was then a simple matter to establish the diamond suit with a ruff and return to dummy with the remaining high spade. Declarer discarded his spade loser on a good diamond and claimed the contract.

After East's raise to 4♡, there was very little chance that he would hold only three hearts. (If he did, and could therefore be fairly sure that a heart would stand up, it would have been his duty to cash the ♡A at Trick 2. It is better to ensure the defeat of the contract, rather than try for two ruffs and a second undertrick.)

If declarer is void in hearts, as you expect, there is still a chance of defeating the contract. Switch to a spade while the diamond suit is blocked! With only one entry to dummy remaining, declarer will not be able to enjoy any discards on the diamond suit. You will need to find your partner with the ♠J, yes, but if declarer has that card (and the expected heart void) he can always make the contract.

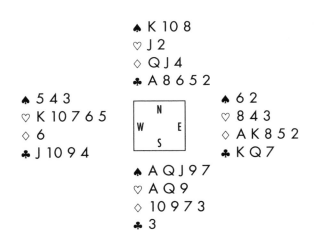

| WEST | NORTH | EAST | SOUTH |
|------|-------|------|-------|
|      |       | 1◇   | 1♠    |
| pass | 2◇*   | pass | 3♠    |
| pass | 4♠    | all pass |   |

*Sitting West, you lead the ◇6 against South's spade game. Partner wins with the king and cashes the ace of diamonds, to which declarer follows with the ◇3 and the ◇7. Partner then leads the ◇2 and declarer plays the ◇9 from his hand. You ruff to give the defenders the first three tricks. How should you continue?*

Partner's ◇2 is a suit preference signal suggesting values in clubs rather than hearts. Should you therefore switch to clubs? That's what West did at the table but he soon regretted it. Declarer won with dummy's ♣A and ruffed a club with the ♠7. He then led the ♠9 to dummy's ten and ruffed another club with the ♠J. The ♠Q to the ♠K revealed that the outstanding trumps were 2-2 after West's ruff. Declarer ruffed a club with the ace, setting up a long club in dummy. He cashed the ◇10, throwing a heart from dummy, played the ♡A and ruffed a heart with dummy's last trump. Trick 13 was then taken with the established ♣8.

West's club switch was pointless, since declarer could not dispose of any club loser that he might have. The only winning defense is to switch to a trump at Trick 4, removing an important entry to dummy. Declarer cannot then set up and enjoy the clubs. West will score the setting trick in hearts.

```
            ♠ Q 6 5 2
            ♡ K J
            ◇ 9 7 4 2
            ♣ A 7 4
♠ 3                          ♠ 9 7
♡ 10 8 7 2      N            ♡ Q 9 6 4 3
◇ Q 8 6 3    W     E         ◇ K J 5
♣ Q 10 5 2      S            ♣ J 9 3
            ♠ A K J 10 8 4
            ♡ A 5
            ◇ A 10
            ♣ K 8 6
```

| WEST | NORTH | EAST | SOUTH |
|------|-------|------|-------|
|      |       |      | 1♠ |
| pass | 3♠ | pass | 6♠ |
| all pass | | | |

*The auction seemed reasonable at the time but the resultant slam was a poor one. West led the ♣10 and declarer saw that his only real chance of making twelve tricks was to set up an extra trick in diamonds. He won with the ♣A and called immediately for a low diamond. Sitting East, how should you react to this?*

Not sensing any danger, the original East followed the adage 'second hand plays low' and contributed the ◇5 to the trick. Declarer played the ten from his hand and West won with the queen. Declarer won the second round of clubs with the king, drew trumps and cashed the diamond ace, dropping the jack from East. He then crossed to dummy with the ♡K and ruffed a diamond. Beginning to regret his earlier defence, East saw his ◇K ruffed into oblivion. Dummy's ◇9 was established and declarer had twelve tricks.

Did you foresee what might happen in diamonds? You need to play an honor on the first round, making sure that your honors contribute to the first two rounds of the suit. Declarer cannot then establish an extra diamond trick and will have no way to make the slam.

# Problem 17

★ Lead: ♡K

                    ♠ K Q J 2
                    ♡ A 3
                    ◇ Q 10
                    ♣ A Q 10 8 2

    ♠ 10 6
    ♡ K Q 10 9 5          N
    ◇ K 7 5 3        W         E
    ♣ 5 4                 S

| WEST | NORTH | EAST | SOUTH |
|------|-------|------|-------|
|      |       |      | 1♣ |
| pass | 1♠ | pass | 2♠ |
| pass | 4NT | pass | 5♡ * |
| pass | 6♣ | all pass | |

You lead the ♡K to dummy's ♡A, partner playing the ♡2. Declarer draws trumps in two rounds and plays three rounds of spades, partner following. Declarer then plays the ♡J to your ♡Q. What next?

# Problem 18

★ Lead: ♠K

                    ♠ A 5 4
                    ♡ 8 5 2
                    ◇ K 10 9 5 3 2
                    ♣ 10

    ♠ K Q 9 2
    ♡ Q 9 7 4             N
    ◇ 7             W         E
    ♣ A 8 6 3             S

| WEST | NORTH | EAST | SOUTH |
|------|-------|------|-------|
|      |       |      | 1◇ |
| dbl | 4◇ | 4♠ | 5◇ |
| all pass | | | |

Sitting West, you lead the ♠K. Dummy's ace wins and your partner contributes the ♠3. Declarer crosses to his hand with the ◇A, East following, and leads the ♣4. How will you defend?

# Problem 19

 Lead: ♣7

```
            ♠ Q 2
            ♡ A 8 5
            ◇ 10 8 5 3 2
            ♣ 6 5 4
```

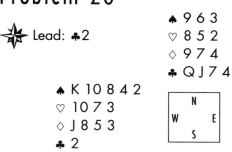

```
                          ♠ 5
                          ♡ 3
                          ◇ A K Q 9 7
                          ♣ A K Q 10 8 3
```

| WEST | NORTH | EAST | SOUTH |
|------|-------|------|-------|
|      |       |      | 1♡ |
| pass | 2♡ | 4NT* | 5♡ |
| pass | pass | dbl | all pass |

West leads the ♣7 (he would lead a second-best ♣7 from ♣9-7-2) and South follows with the ♣J. How will you plan the defense?

# Problem 20

 Lead: ♣2

```
            ♠ 9 6 3
            ♡ 8 5 2
            ◇ 9 7 4
            ♣ Q J 7 4
```

```
♠ K 10 8 4 2
♡ 10 7 3
◇ J 8 5 3
♣ 2
```

| WEST | NORTH | EAST | SOUTH |
|------|-------|------|-------|
|      |       |      | 2♣ |
| pass | 2◇ | pass | 2♡ |
| pass | 3♡ | pass | 3♠ |
| pass | 4♡ | pass | 6♡ |
| all pass |       |      |    |

Declarer wins your club lead with the ace, draws one round of trumps and then surprises you by playing the ♣K. How will you defend?

```
                    ♠ K Q J 2
                    ♡ A 3
                    ◇ Q 10
                    ♣ A Q 10 8 2
   ♠ 10 6                              ♠ 9 5 4
   ♡ K Q 10 9 5        N              ♡ 8 6 2
   ◇ K 7 5 3       W        E         ◇ 9 8 6 4 2
   ♣ 5 4               S              ♣ 9 6
                    ♠ A 8 7 3
                    ♡ J 7 4
                    ◇ A J
                    ♣ K J 7 3
```

| WEST | NORTH | EAST | SOUTH |
|------|-------|------|-------|
|      |       |      | 1♣ |
| pass | 1♠ | pass | 2♠ |
| pass | 4NT | pass | 5♡ * |
| pass | 6♣ | all pass | |

*You lead the ♡K to dummy's ♡A, partner playing the ♡2. Declarer draws trumps in two rounds and plays three rounds of spades, partner following. Declarer then plays the ♡J to your ♡Q. What next?*

As it happens, 6♠ would have been a better contract because South's potential diamond loser can be thrown on the fifth club. Declarer ends in 6♣, however, and you lead the ♡K.

There are two possible lines of play. Declarer could take a simple diamond finesse. Alternatively, he could play you for the diamond king, planning to run all his black-suit winners and endplay you with a heart to lead into the diamond tenace.

The original declarer aimed to avoid a guess by deception. He won the heart lead and drew trumps in two rounds. After cashing three rounds of spades, eliminating that suit, he led the jack of hearts to

West's queen. By leading the jack, he hoped to give the impression that this was his last heart. Suppose you had been West. What would you have done next?

Fearing that declarer had no more hearts, the original West was reluctant to concede a ruff-and-sluff. He switched to a low diamond, hoping that East held the jack and that declarer would misguess. Declarer then had twelve tricks.

Such a deception is easily unmasked by a count signal from East at Trick 1. The ♡2 shows an odd number of hearts. When declarer subsequently leads the ♡J, you know that South and East both started with three hearts. You therefore know that a third round of hearts will be safe. Declarer ruffs in the dummy and has to take the diamond finesse. Down one!

```
                    ♠ A 5 4
                    ♡ 8 5 2
                    ◇ K 10 9 5 3 2
                    ♣ 10
      ♠ K Q 9 2       ┌─────────┐      ♠ J 10 8 7 3
      ♡ Q 9 7 4       │    N    │      ♡ K 10 3
      ◇ 7             │ W     E │      ◇ 8
      ♣ A 8 6 3       │    S    │      ♣ K 7 5 2
                      └─────────┘
                    ♠ 6
                    ♡ A J 6
                    ◇ A Q J 6 4
                    ♣ Q J 9 4
```

| WEST | NORTH | EAST | SOUTH |
|------|-------|------|-------|
|      |       |      | 1◇    |
| dbl  | 4◇    | 4♠   | 5◇    |
| all pass |    |      |       |

*Sitting West, you lead the ♠K against South's diamond game. Dummy's ace wins the trick and your partner contributes the ♠3. Declarer crosses to his hand with the ◇A, East following, and leads the ♣4. How will you defend?*

You must rise with the club ace. It is tempting to think that partner may be able to win cheaply with the jack or queen but if declarer's clubs were headed by the king he would doubtless have led the suit from dummy. If you carelessly play low on the first round of clubs, partner will win with the king but your ace will then be subject to a ruffing finesse. Declarer will set up two club winners on which to throw dummy's heart losers and will emerge with an overtrick.

So, you win with the ♣A. What next? Is a spade trick available for the defense? No. Partner's ♠3 at Trick 1 was a count signal in response to your lead of a king. He has an odd number of spades, which can only be five on the bidding. You can beat the contract only by scoring one club trick and two heart tricks. You must therefore switch to hearts now, before declarer establishes a winner or two in clubs. Your low heart switch goes to partner's king and declarer's ace. The hard work has been done. Struggle as he may, declarer will not be able to avoid the loss of one club and two hearts.

```
              ♠ Q 2
              ♡ A 8 5
              ◇ 10 8 5 3 2
              ♣ 6 5 4
♠ 10 9 8 7 3                      ♠ 5
♡ J 9 2          N                ♡ 3
◇ J 6 4       W     E             ◇ A K Q 9 7
♣ 7 2            S                ♣ A K Q 10 8 3
              ♠ A K J 6 4
              ♡ K Q 10 7 6 4
              ◇ —
              ♣ J 9
```

| WEST | NORTH | EAST | SOUTH |
|------|-------|------|-------|
|      |       |      | 1♡ |
| pass | 2♡ | 4NT | 5♡ |
| pass | pass | dbl | all pass |

*You are sitting East and your 4NT was an example of the Unusual Notrump, showing two long minor suits. South decided to try his luck in 5♡ and your double ended the auction. West, your partner, leads the ♣7. You win with the queen of clubs and declarer follows with the jack. How will you continue the defense?*

You have no way of reading the club position. You partner could have led the seven from ♣9-7-2, ♣7-2 or a singleton ♣7. What you do know, though, is that declarer cannot possibly get rid of any diamond losers. Consequently there is no need whatsoever to switch to diamonds at this stage. You persist with the ace of clubs and both the closed hands follow suit. What next? Again there is no possible reason to play a diamond. If declarer has one or more diamond losers, he cannot dispose of them. You have nothing to lose by playing a third club and this promotes a trump trick for your partner, putting the doubled contract one down.

If you play a diamond at Trick 2 or Trick 3, declarer makes the contract by drawing two rounds of trumps and testing the spades. They break 5-1 but he can ruff the third round in dummy.

```
                    ♠ 9 6 3
                    ♡ 8 5 2
                    ◇ 9 7 4
                    ♣ Q J 7 4
    ♠ K 10 8 4 2        ┌─────────┐        ♠ J 7 5
    ♡ 10 7 3            │    N    │        ♡ 6
    ◇ J 8 5 3          │ W     E │        ◇ Q 10 2
    ♣ 2                │    S    │        ♣ 10 9 8 6 5 3
                       └─────────┘
                    ♠ A Q
                    ♡ A K Q J 9 4
                    ◇ A K 6
                    ♣ A K
```

| WEST | NORTH | EAST | SOUTH |
|------|-------|------|-------|
|      |       |      | 2♣    |
| pass | 2◇    | pass | 2♡    |
| pass | 3♡    | pass | 3♠    |
| pass | 4♡    | pass | 6♡    |
| all pass | | | |

*Sitting West, you lead your singleton club against South's small slam in hearts. Declarer wins with the ♣A and draws one round of trumps with the ace. He then surprises you by playing the ♣K. How will you defend?*

What possible reason can South have for playing another top club before drawing trumps? If he held ♣A-K-x he would surely draw trumps and then score four club tricks. So, it seems that he has ♣A-K and the club suit is blocked. Should you ruff this second round of clubs? No, because dummy's ♡8 would then become an entry. Declarer would be able to draw your last trump with the ♡K and lead the ♡4 to dummy's ♡8. He could then throw two losers on the ♣Q-J. You refuse to ruff, therefore, and declarer tests you again by leading the ♡9. How will you defend?

If you win with the ♡10 declarer will again be able to cross to dummy with the ♡8. So, you must allow South's ♡9 to win the trick. Declarer's only remaining chance is to cash his red-suit winners, hoping that a defender will reduce to ♠K-x ◇Q and can then be thrown in. This rescue attempt will fail and the slam tumbles to defeat.

# Problem 21

 Lead: ◇Q

```
            ♠ Q 9 2
            ♡ A 10 9 4
            ◇ K 5
            ♣ K 8 4 2
                        ♠ K 10
         N              ♡ K 6 5
    W         E         ◇ A 9 8 4 3
         S              ♣ J 10 6
```

| WEST | NORTH | EAST | SOUTH |
|------|-------|------|-------|
|      | 1♣    | pass | 1♠    |
| pass | 2♠    | pass | 4♠    |
| all pass |    |      |       |

The ◇Q wins and partner plays a second diamond to your ace. Where will you find two further tricks?

# Problem 22

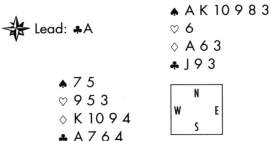 Lead: ♣A

```
                  ♠ A K 10 9 8 3
                  ♡ 6
                  ◇ A 6 3
                  ♣ J 9 3
    ♠ 7 5
    ♡ 9 5 3               N
    ◇ K 10 9 4       W         E
    ♣ A 7 6 4             S
```

| WEST | NORTH | EAST | SOUTH |
|------|-------|------|-------|
|      | 1♠    | pass | 2♡    |
| pass | 2♠    | pass | 4NT   |
| pass | 5◇*   | pass | 6♡    |
| all pass |   |      |       |

Sitting West, you lead the ♣A. Partner plays an encouraging ♣8 and the ♣K appears from South. What now?

# Problem 23

 Lead: ◇8

♠ A Q 3
♡ A Q J 3
◇ Q
♣ A K Q J 6

♠ 8 4
♡ 10 8 2
◇ A K 6 2
♣ 10 9 5 4

| WEST | NORTH | EAST | SOUTH |
|------|-------|------|-------|
|      | 2♣    | pass | 2◇    |
| pass | 3♣    | pass | 3♠    |
| pass | 4♠    | pass | 5♠    |
| pass | 6♠    | all pass |   |

West leads the ◇8 (second best from a poor suit). Sitting East, you win with the ◇K. What is your plan for the defense?

# Problem 24

 Lead: ♡Q

♠ K J 8 3
♡ 7 5 4
◇ A J 8
♣ A 8 4

♠ 9 7 2
♡ A J 9 6 3
◇ K 10 3
♣ K 2

| WEST | NORTH | EAST | SOUTH |
|------|-------|------|-------|
|      |       | 1♡   | dbl   |
| pass | 2♡    | pass | 2♠    |
| pass | 4♠    | all pass |   |

Sitting East, you allow partner's ♡Q to run to South's ♡K. Declarer draws trumps in three rounds, your partner throwing the ♣3 on the third round, and exits with the ♡10, partner following with the ♡8. How will you defend?

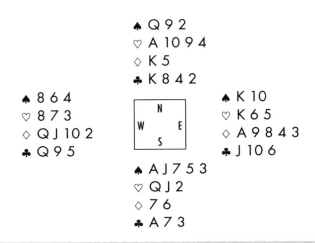

| WEST | NORTH | EAST | SOUTH |
|------|-------|------|-------|
|      | 1♣    | pass | 1♠    |
| pass | 2♠    | pass | 4♠    |
| all pass | | | |

*Your partner wins the first trick with the ◇ Q and plays a second diamond to your ace. Where will you find two further tricks?*

When the deal was originally played, East switched to the ♣J at Trick 2. Declarer won with dummy's ♣K and played a low trump to the ten and jack. The jack won and the ace of trumps then dropped East's king. Playing safe, declarer drew West's last trump with the queen and led a low heart from dummy. East could win the first or second round of hearts but declarer would then claim the remainder. He would score five trump tricks, three hearts and two diamonds.

How can you do better in the East seat? You should try the effect of playing the king on the first round of trumps! If declarer reads this as a singleton, he will win with the ace and finesse dummy's ♠9 on the second round. You will win with the ♠10, trying not to look smug, and exit safely in diamonds. When an eventual heart finesse loses, the game will be down one.

```
                    ♠ A K 10 9 8 3
                    ♡ 6
                    ◊ A 6 3
                    ♣ J 9 3
  ♠ 7 5                           ♠ Q 6 2
  ♡ 9 5 3          ┌─────────┐    ♡ 7 4 2
  ◊ K 10 9 4       │    N    │    ◊ 7 5
  ♣ A 7 6 4     W  │         │  E ♣ Q 10 8 5 2
                   │    S    │
                   └─────────┘
                    ♠ J 4
                    ♡ A K Q J 10 8
                    ◊ Q J 8 2
                    ♣ K
```

| WEST | NORTH | EAST | SOUTH |
|------|-------|------|-------|
|  | 1♠ | pass | 2♡ |
| pass | 2♠ | pass | 4NT |
| pass | 5◊* | pass | 6♡ |
| all pass | | | |

*South should have bid 3◊ at his second turn rather than a clumsy RKCB bid. North's 5◊ response showed three keycards, with spades temporarily agreed as trumps, and his partner closed the auction in 6♡. Sitting West, you decide to lead the ♣A. Partner plays an encouraging ♣8 and the ♣K appears from South. What now?*

At the table West continued with a 'safe' second round of clubs. This was very much to declarer's liking. He ruffed in his hand and drew trumps in three rounds. He then took the percentage play in spades, cashing the ace-king and ruffing a third round of the suit. When the spades broke 3-2, declarer re-entered dummy with the ◊A and discarded his three diamond losers on the established spades. Slam made!

What could West have done about it? One possibility was to switch to the ◊10 (or the ◊9) at Trick 2. Fearing the loss of two quick tricks, declarer might then have won with the diamond ace, drawn trumps and run the ♠J in the hope that he could bring in the whole spade suit.

An even better defense was for West to switch to the ◇K at Trick 2. This would knock out the dummy's side entry for certain, leaving declarer with no chance of making the contract.

```
              ♠ A Q 3
              ♡ A Q J 3
              ◇ Q
              ♣ A K Q J 6
♠ J 9 6          ┌─────────┐          ♠ 8 4
♡ K 7 5 4        │    N    │          ♡ 10 8 2
◇ 9 8 7 3      W │         │ E        ◇ A K 6 2
♣ 8 3            │    S    │          ♣ 10 9 5 4
                 └─────────┘
              ♠ K 10 7 5 2
              ♡ 9 6
              ◇ J 10 5 4
              ♣ 7 2
```

| WEST | NORTH | EAST | SOUTH |
|------|-------|------|-------|
|  | 2♣ | pass | 2◇ |
| pass | 3♣ | pass | 3♠ |
| pass | 4♠ | pass | 5♠ |
| pass | 6♠ | all pass | |

*West leads the ◇8 (second-best from a poor suit) against South's small slam in spades. Sitting East, you win with the ◇K. What is your plan for the defense?*

Prospects of a trick in hearts or clubs are non-existent. There is, however, a significant chance that your side will score a trump trick. At Trick 2 you must continue with the ◇A, forcing dummy to ruff. Declarer will continue with the ace and queen of trumps, both defenders following. He must then reach his hand to draw the last trump. The only prospect of achieving this is to ruff the third round of clubs. Unlucky! West overruffs with the ♠J and the slam is down one.

This defense would also succeed in the less likely situation where West holds ♠K-x-x and South has bid 5♠ with ♠J-10-x-x-x and the ♡K. After ruffing in the dummy, declarer would no longer be able to take two finesses against the trump king.

```
                    ♠ K J 8 3
                    ♡ 7 5 4
                    ◇ A J 8
                    ♣ A 8 4
   ♠ 6 4                              ♠ 9 7 2
   ♡ Q 8              ┌─────────┐     ♡ A J 9 6 3
   ◇ 7 6 5 2          │   N     │     ◇ K 10 3
   ♣ 10 9 7 6 3       │ W     E │     ♣ K 2
                      │   S     │
                      └─────────┘
                    ♠ A Q 10 5
                    ♡ K 10 2
                    ◇ Q 9 4
                    ♣ Q J 5
```

| WEST | NORTH | EAST | SOUTH |
|------|-------|------|-------|
|      |       | 1 ♡  | dbl   |
| pass | 2 ♡   | pass | 2 ♠   |
| pass | 4 ♠   | all pass | |

*You are sitting East and your partner leads the ♡Q against South's spade game. How will you defend?*

The first point to note is that you should not play your ♡A on the first trick. This would promote South's remaining ♡K-10 into two tricks. You allow South to win the first trick with the ♡K and he draws trumps in three rounds, your partner discarding the ♣3 on the third round. Declarer now exits with the ♡10, your partner playing the ♡8. How will you continue the defense?

Since you have no wish to be thrown in a second time, you should cash your remaining heart trick. Your next play is more difficult and will require some thought. What is declarer's shape? Your partner's discard of the ♣3 (a low spot-card) tells you that he started with an odd number of clubs. He surely has five clubs, leaving declarer with 4-3-3-3 shape. In that case South is likely to have a respectable point-count for his double. In particular, you can expect him to hold both the minor-suit queens.

What will happen if you exit with a diamond now? Declarer will win with the ◇Q or the ◇J and continue with ace and another club. You will be endplayed again and have to give declarer two more diamond tricks or concede a ruff-and-sluff. Either way, the contract will be made.

If instead you exit with a club, you will give declarer three club tricks when he holds the queen and jack of the suit. The only safe return is a fourth round of hearts, deliberately conceding a ruff-and-sluff. Declarer has no answer to this. Suppose he ruffs in his hand and throws one diamond from the dummy. He can continue with ace and another club, throwing you in again, but now you play a fifth round of hearts. Declarer ruffs with his last trump and you will score a diamond trick to defeat the contract.

Even though you could deduce almost exactly what hand declarer held, it was still quite hard work to calculate the best defense. There are two ways of looking at this. It's bad news, of course, that you have to put in so much effort. The good news is that few players are willing to do the same. If you are determined to go the extra mile yourself, you can leap-frog over them!

# Problem 25

 Lead: ♡8

♠ K J 5
♡ 7 4 3
◇ A Q J 10
♣ K Q 6

♠ 7
♡ A K Q J 6 5
◇ 8 6 4 3
♣ A 8

| WEST | NORTH | EAST | SOUTH |
|------|-------|------|-------|
|      |       | 1♡   | 1♠    |
| pass | 2♡*   | 3♡   | pass  |
| pass | 4♠    | all pass |    |

You win partner's ♡8 with the ♡J and continue with the ♡A, everyone following. South ruffs the ♡K with the ♠10 and West throws the ◇7. How will you defend when declarer plays a club to dummy's king?

# Problem 26

 Lead: ◇9

♠ A K 8 2
♡ 8 3
◇ K 6
♣ A K Q 6 2

♠ Q 4
♡ K Q J 2
◇ A Q 3 2
♣ J 8 3

| WEST | NORTH | EAST | SOUTH |
|------|-------|------|-------|
|      |       | 1NT  | pass  |
| 2◇*  | 2♡*   | 3♡   | 3♠    |
| pass | 4♠    | all pass |    |

Your partner's 2◇ was a transfer bid, showing hearts, and North's 2♡ was for take-out. How will you defend when West leads the ◇9 and declarer plays low from dummy?

# Problem 27

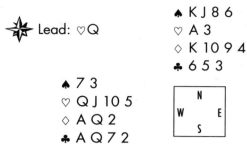

Lead: ♡Q

♠ K J 8 6
♡ A 3
◇ K 10 9 4
♣ 6 5 3

♠ 7 3
♡ Q J 10 5
◇ A Q 2
♣ A Q 7 2

| WEST | NORTH | EAST | SOUTH |
|------|-------|------|-------|
|      |       |      | 1♠    |
| dbl  | 2NT*  | pass | 3♠    |
| pass | 4♠    | all pass |   |

Sitting West, you lead the ♡Q. Declarer wins with dummy's ♡A and your partner discourages with the ♡2. Declarer plays a trump to the queen and leads a low diamond towards dummy. How will you defend?

# Problem 28

Lead: ♠3

♠ K J 8 4
♡ J 4
◇ 7
♣ J 9 8 7 4 2

♠ 3
♡ K 10 9 2
◇ A Q 8 5
♣ K Q 10 5

| WEST | NORTH | EAST | SOUTH |
|------|-------|------|-------|
|      |       | 3♠   | 4♡    |
| dbl  | all pass |   |       |

You lead the ♠3, East winning dummy's ♠8 with the ♠9. Declarer wins the ♣6 return with the ace and advances the ◇2. What is your plan to extract a maximum penalty?

♠ K J 5
♡ 7 4 3
◇ A Q J 10
♣ K Q 6

♠ 9 8 6 4
♡ 8 2
◇ 7 5
♣ J 10 7 5 2

```
      N
   W     E
      S
```

♠ 7
♡ A K Q J 6 5
◇ 8 6 4 3
♣ A 8

♠ A Q 10 3 2
♡ 10 9
◇ K 9 2
♣ 9 4 3

| WEST | NORTH | EAST | SOUTH |
|------|-------|------|-------|
|      |       | 1♡   | 1♠    |
| pass | 2♡*   | 3♡   | pass  |
| pass | 4♠    | all pass |    |

*You are sitting East and partner leads the ♡8 against South's spade game. You win with the jack of hearts and continue with the ace, everyone following. What now?*

It is fairly obvious to continue with a third top heart, aiming to promote partner's trump holding. Declarer ruffs with the ♠10 and your partner discards the ◇7. Declarer's next move is a club to the king. How will you defend from this point?

There is no conceivable reason to duck. Indeed, if you do hold up the ♣A declarer will draw trumps and run four diamond tricks for the contract. Instead you should win with the ♣A and play a fourth round of hearts, deliberately giving a ruff-and-sluff. Declarer cannot afford to ruff in his hand because this will leave him with fewer trumps than West. He will discard his losing club and ruff with dummy's ♠5. Your partner, meanwhile, will throw his last diamond. When declarer cashes dummy's king of spades, followed by the jack, you will show out on the second round. Knowing that he cannot afford to overtake, declarer will follow with a low trump and then attempt to reach his hand with a diamond to the king. Not today, my friend! Your partner will ruff the first round of diamonds, defeating the contract.

# SOLUTION TO PROBLEM 26

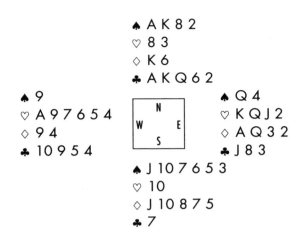

|  ♠ A K 8 2 |
|  ♡ 8 3 |
|  ◇ K 6 |
|  ♣ A K Q 6 2 |

| WEST | NORTH | EAST | SOUTH |
|------|-------|------|-------|
|      |       | 1NT  | pass  |
| 2◇*  | 2♡*   | 3♡   | 3♠    |
| pass | 4♠    | all pass |   |

*Sitting East, you open 1NT and West's 2◇ is a transfer response that shows at least five hearts. North bids 2♡, the opponents' suit, for take-out and South ends in 4♠. How will you defend the contract when West leads the ◇9 and declarer plays low from dummy?*

Since your partner would lead second-best from a bad suit (for example, the ◇7 from ◇ 9-7-6-4), the lead of a nine implies a single-ton or doubleton. You win the first trick with the diamond queen and cash the ace of diamonds, West following with the ◇4. What now?

You must hope that partner holds the ♡A. If he has only five hearts you will be able to take two heart tricks, defeating the contract. If instead partner holds six hearts, you will have only one heart trick to take. Your only remaining chance of a setting trick will be to lead another diamond, hoping that partner has a big enough trump to dis-lodge one of dummy's honors.

To discover how many hearts partner holds, you request a count signal by leading the ♡K. When partner plays the ♡7, you know that he holds six hearts. You therefore switch back to diamonds. Partner ruffs with the ♠9, dummy overruffs with the ♠K and your ♠Q is promoted into the setting trick. If partner had given you a low count signal, showing five hearts, you would have played a second round of hearts instead.

```
              ♠ K J 8 6
              ♡ A 3
              ◇ K 10 9 4
              ♣ 6 5 3
♠ 7 3                        ♠ 4 2
♡ Q J 10 5      N           ♡ 8 7 6 2
◇ A Q 2      W     E        ◇ J 8 6 5
♣ A Q 7 2       S           ♣ J 10 9
              ♠ A Q 10 9 5
              ♡ K 9 4
              ◇ 7 3
              ♣ K 8 4
```

| WEST | NORTH | EAST | SOUTH |
|------|-------|------|-------|
|      |       |      | 1♠ |
| dbl | 2NT* | pass | 3♠ |
| pass | 4♠ | all pass | |

*North's decision to bid game was pushy but when the opponents bid forwardly, you must be on your toes in defense. Sitting West, you lead the ♡Q. Declarer wins with dummy's ♡A, your partner playing the ♡2. Declarer plays a trump to the queen and leads a low diamond towards dummy. How will you defend?*

Partner's ♡2 on the first trick was an attitude signal denying the ♡K. (Remember that our recommended signaling method is to signal attitude on an ace or queen lead and count on a king lead.) To beat the contract you will need one diamond trick and three club tricks. Unless South has opened very light, he will hold the ♣K. Your best hope is therefore that partner has the ◇J. Provided you defend correctly, partner will win a trick with it and can then switch to a club.

Suppose you rise with the ◇A on the first round. You can exit safely in hearts or trumps but declarer will be able to eliminate the diamonds with two ruffs. He can then play the ♡K and the ♡9, throwing a club loser from dummy as you win the third round. You will be end-played, forced to give a ruff-and-sluff or lead away from the ♣A.

What if you follow with the ◇2 on the first round? Declarer will win with dummy's king and you will be forced to win the second round of diamonds with the ace or queen. Once again declarer will be able to eliminate diamonds and throw you in with a heart. The only successful defense is to play the queen of diamonds on the first round. East can then win the second round of diamonds with the jack and switch to the ♣J. Down one!

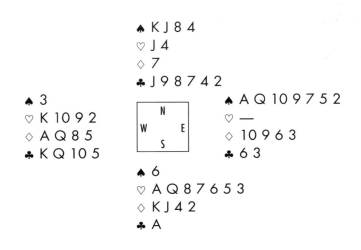

|  | ♠ K J 8 4 |  |
|  | ♡ J 4 |  |
|  | ◇ 7 |  |
|  | ♣ J 9 8 7 4 2 |  |

♠ 3               ♠ A Q 10 9 7 5 2
♡ K 10 9 2        ♡ —
◇ A Q 8 5         ◇ 10 9 6 3
♣ K Q 10 5        ♣ 6 3

|  | ♠ 6 |  |
|  | ♡ A Q 8 7 6 5 3 |  |
|  | ◇ K J 4 2 |  |
|  | ♣ A |  |

| WEST | NORTH | EAST | SOUTH |
|------|-------|------|-------|
|      |       | 3♠   | 4♡    |
| dbl  | all pass |   |       |

*You double South's 4♡ overcall and lead your singleton spade, East winning with the ♠9 over dummy's ♠8. Declarer wins the ♣6 return with the ace and advances the ◇2. How will you defend?*

Declarer is clearly planning a diamond ruff or two. How can you stop him? You would rather a trump lead came from partner. Should you therefore play low on the first diamond, hoping that partner can win and return a trump? It's not a promising defense. Partner can see as well as you can that declarer might score some diamond ruffs. If partner held a trump he would have returned it at Trick 2.

Your best play is to step in with the ◇8, winning the trick. What now? If you play a top club declarer will score two diamond ruffs. He can then endplay you twice in the red suits, escaping for just one down. Suppose you follow the stronger defense of returning the ♡10. The contract will now go two down. Declarer will score one diamond ruff in dummy and will then endplay you twice, as before. Can you do any better than this?

Indeed you can. After winning with the ◇8 you should return the king of trumps! Declarer wins with the trump ace. If he now takes a diamond ruff with the jack, your remaining 10-9-2 in the trump suit will be worth two tricks. Declarer will lose one spade, three diamonds and two trumps, going three down. Nor will he fare any better by declining to ruff a diamond.

# Problem 29

 Lead: ♣Q

♠ J 10 7 5
♡ A 4
◇ K Q 9 6
♣ 8 7 2

♠ Q 8 6
♡ 10 7 3
◇ 10 3
♣ A K J 10 9

| WEST | NORTH | EAST | SOUTH |
|------|-------|------|-------|
|      |       |      | 1NT |
| pass | 2♣ | dbl | 2♠ |
| pass | 4♠ | all pass |  |

Your double showed clubs. You overtake the ♣Q and cash two more clubs, partner throwing a diamond on the third round. What now?

# Problem 30

 Lead: ♣2

♠ A Q J
♡ 7 4 3
◇ A K 5
♣ K J 7 3

♠ 10 9 8 6 2
♡ Q 9
◇ 9 7 2
♣ A Q 6

| WEST | NORTH | EAST | SOUTH |
|------|-------|------|-------|
|      | 1♣ | pass | 1♡ |
| pass | 2NT | pass | 3◇ |
| pass | 3♡ | pass | 4♡ |
| all pass |  |  |  |

West leads the ♣2 against South's heart game. Declarer plays the jack from dummy and you win with the club queen. What now?

# Problem 31

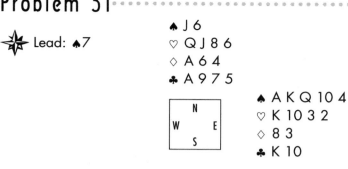

♣ Lead: ♠7

```
      ♠ J 6
      ♡ Q J 8 6
      ◇ A 6 4
      ♣ A 9 7 5
                    ♠ A K Q 10 4
        N           ♡ K 10 3 2
     W     E        ◇ 8 3
        S           ♣ K 10
```

| WEST | NORTH | EAST | SOUTH |
|------|-------|------|-------|
|      |       | 1♠   | 2◇    |
| 3♠   | dbl*  | pass | 4♡    |
| all pass |    |      |       |

West's 3♠ bid was preemptive. You win the spade lead and cash a second spade trick, South following suit. What now?

# Problem 32

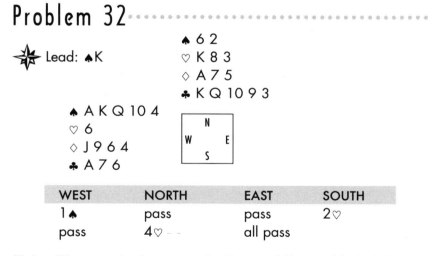

♣ Lead: ♠K

```
                ♠ 6 2
                ♡ K 8 3
                ◇ A 7 5
                ♣ K Q 10 9 3
  ♠ A K Q 10 4
  ♡ 6                   N
  ◇ J 9 6 4        W         E
  ♣ A 7 6               S
```

| WEST | NORTH | EAST | SOUTH |
|------|-------|------|-------|
| 1♠   | pass  | pass | 2♡    |
| pass | 4♡    | all pass |   |

Sitting West, you lead a top spade. Partner follows with the ♠3, suggesting a three-card spade holding. How will you continue?

```
                     ♠ J 10 7 5
                     ♡ A 4
                     ◇ K Q 9 6
                     ♣ 8 7 2
  ♠ 9 3                                   ♠ Q 8 6
  ♡ Q J 8 5 2         ┌─────────┐         ♡ 10 7 3
  ◇ 7 5 4 2           │    N    │         ◇ 10 3
  ♣ Q 5             W │ W     E │ E       ♣ A K J 10 9
                      │    S    │
                      └─────────┘
                     ♠ A K 4 2
                     ♡ K 9 6
                     ◇ A J 8
                     ♣ 6 4 3
```

| WEST | NORTH | EAST | SOUTH |
|------|-------|------|-------|
|      |       |      | 1NT |
| pass | 2♣ | dbl | 2♠ |
| pass | 4♠ | all pass | |

*Sitting East, you double the 2♣ Stayman bid to suggest a club lead. Partner duly leads the ♣Q against four spades. You overtake and cash two more clubs successfully, partner throwing a diamond on the third round. What now?*

Only 18 points are missing and South's 1NT opening advertised 15-17 points. Declarer is therefore marked with the ◇A and at least the ♡K or the ♡Q-J and it will not be possible to score a further trick from the side suits. You should therefore lead a fourth round of clubs. It makes no difference that this will give declarer a ruff-and-sluff, since he has no loser to throw. You hope that partner can ruff with the ♠9, forcing dummy to overruff with the ten or the jack. Your ♠Q-8-6 will then be worth a trick and the contract will go down one.

Without the point-count information provided by South's 1NT opening, such a defense would be risky. Declarer might hold the ♠9 and perhaps only a queen in the heart suit. He would then be able to ruff the fourth round of clubs with the ♠9 and discard dummy's heart loser. A subsequent trump finesse would then land the contract.

```
                    ♠ A Q J
                    ♡ 7 4 3
                    ◇ A K 5
                    ♣ K J 7 3
   ♠ K 7 5 3                          ♠ 10 9 8 6 2
   ♡ K 8 2           ┌─────────┐      ♡ Q 9
   ◇ J 4             │    N    │      ◇ 9 7 2
   ♣ 10 8 5 2        │  W   E  │      ♣ A Q 6
                     │    S    │
                     └─────────┘
                    ♠ 4
                    ♡ A J 10 6 5
                    ◇ Q 10 8 6 3
                    ♣ 9 4
```

| WEST | NORTH | EAST | SOUTH |
|------|-------|------|-------|
|  | 1♣ | pass | 1♡ |
| pass | 2NT | pass | 3◇ |
| pass | 3♡ | pass | 4♡ |
| all pass |  |  |  |

*West, your partner, has no attractive lead against South's heart game. He eventually opts for the ♣2, which will prove a lucky choice provided you can defend strongly thereafter in the East seat. Declarer plays the jack from the dummy and you win with the club queen. What now?*

Prospects of a trick in spades or diamonds are not bright. It is best to hope for two club tricks and two trump tricks. You should cash the ♣A at Trick 2 and continue with a third round of clubs. Declarer now has no way of avoiding two trump losers. If he plays ace and another trump, you and partner will score your trump honors separately. If instead declarer finesses the ♡J on the first round, West will win with the ♡K and lead a fourth round of clubs. You will ruff with the now singleton ♡Q, promoting West's ♡8 into the setting trick.

```
                        ♠ J 6
                        ♡ Q J 8 6
                        ◇ A 6 4
                        ♣ A 9 7 5
     ♠ 8 7 5 3                              ♠ A K Q 10 4
     ♡ 7               ┌─────────┐          ♡ K 10 3 2
     ◇ J 9            W│   N     │E         ◇ 8 3
     ♣ J 8 6 4 3 2     │   S     │          ♣ K 10
                       └─────────┘
                        ♠ 9 2
                        ♡ A 9 5 4
                        ◇ K Q 10 7 5 2
                        ♣ Q
```

| WEST | NORTH | EAST | SOUTH |
|------|-------|------|-------|
|      |       | 1♠   | 2◇    |
| 3♠   | dbl*  | pass | 4♡    |
| all pass |    |      |       |

*West leaps preemptively to 3♠ in an effort to shut out the heart suit. (With a sound raise to 3♠ he would have cuebid 3◇ instead.) North has a perfect hand for a competitive double and the heart game is reached. West leads the ♠7 and, sitting East, you win with the ♠10. A second spade stands up, your partner following with the ♠3 to show that he began with four spades. What now?*

South is likely to be 4-6 in the red suits, which will leave him with only one club. You cannot hope to score a trick with the ♣K and will therefore need to make two trump tricks. To achieve this, you must play a third round of spades now, deliberately conceding a ruff-and-sluff. Declarer has no counter to this defense, whichever hand he chooses to ruff in. When you gain the lead later in trumps, you intend to attack the trump length in the other hand, setting up a long trump for yourself.

Let's assume that declarer ruffs in the dummy and plays the ♡Q. You must not cover! If you do, declarer will win with the ♡A and play a heart to dummy's eight. You will have to take your trump trick; dummy's ♡J can then deal with a fourth round of spades. (Declarer's ♡9-5 will later draw your ♡3-2.) So, let the ♡Q pass. If declarer plays another trump from dummy, you will cover to force South's ace. When you win the third round of trumps, you can force the South hand and promote a second trump trick for yourself.

Suppose next that declarer chooses to ruff the third spade in his hand. He crosses to the ♣A and leads the ♡Q. You do not need to defend so precisely now. The contract will go down whether you cover or not. You will gain the lead on the third round of trumps and can then force the dummy's trump length with a fourth round of spades.

This deal is a variation of a well-known type where a defender holds A-x-x-x in the trump suit. Suppose, sitting East, you held ♡A-6-3-2 instead. You would again give a ruff-and-sluff at Trick 3. When declarer played trumps you would hold up your ace until the third round. Since there would now be no trumps in the hand where declarer had taken the spade force, you would be able to force the other hand with a fourth round of spades. Once again you would set up a second trump trick for yourself, thereby beating the contract.

```
                          ♠ 6 2
                          ♡ K 8 3
                          ◇ A 7 5
                          ♣ K Q 10 9 3
     ♠ A K Q 10 4                              ♠ J 8 3
     ♡ 6                    ┌─────────┐        ♡ 10 9 7 4
     ◇ J 9 6 4            W │    N    │ E      ◇ Q 10 8 3
     ♣ A 7 6               │    S    │        ♣ 8 4
                            └─────────┘
                          ♠ 9 7 5
                          ♡ A Q J 5 2
                          ◇ K 2
                          ♣ J 5 2
```

| WEST | NORTH | EAST | SOUTH |
|------|-------|------|-------|
| 1♠ | pass | pass | 2♡ |
| pass | 4♡ | all pass | |

*Sitting West, you lead the ♠K. Partner follows with the ♠3, suggesting a three-card spade holding. How will you continue?*

You expect to score three top tricks in the black suits. Where can you find a fourth trick? If partner holds the ◇K, a diamond switch will work well. You will set up a diamond trick before declarer has a chance to discard his diamond losers on dummy's club suit. Who is more likely to hold the ◇K, though — East, who could not find a response to a one-bid, or South, who showed good values with a two-level balancing overcall?

When the deal arose in the 2004 Spingold semifinals, Lorenzo Lauria of Italy concluded that South was likely to hold the ◇K. He knew that if he continued with a second top spade, declarer would be able to ruff his third spade in the dummy, losing just three black-suit tricks. The same would happen if he switched to a red suit. Lauria could see one remaining chance — that his partner held a doubleton club. He made the brilliant switch of a low club!

What could declarer do? If he conceded a spade trick, preparing for a spade ruff, West would win and give his partner a club ruff. If instead declarer drew trumps and played another club, West would win and cash two more spade tricks.

A big swing to Lauria's team, was it? No, at the other table the mighty Bob Hamman of the USA found exactly the same defense!

# Problem 33

 Lead: ♣K

♠ K 4 3
♡ A 6 2
◇ A 8 7 5 2
♣ 8 4

♠ 8 2
♡ J 10
◇ K Q J 9
♣ A K Q J 3

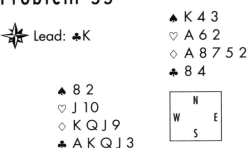

| WEST | NORTH | EAST | SOUTH |
|------|-------|------|-------|
|      |       |      | 1♠    |
| 2♣   | 2◇    | pass | 2♠    |
| pass | 4♠    | all pass |   |

You lead the ♣K followed by the ♣A. East plays the ♣7 followed by the ♣2; declarer plays the ♣5 and the ♣10. How will you continue?

# Problem 34

 Lead: ◇J

♠ A 10 4 2
♡ K Q
◇ A K 3 2
♣ J 8 5

♠ Q J 8
♡ J 9 7 4
◇ 8 4
♣ Q 10 4 2

| WEST | NORTH | EAST | SOUTH |
|------|-------|------|-------|
|      |       |      | 1NT   |
| pass | 2♣    | pass | 2♠    |
| pass | 6♠    | all pass |   |

Declarer wins with the ◇A, plays the ♠A-K and the ♡A-K. He then continues with the queen and king of diamonds. What is your plan?

# Problem 35

 Lead: ♡K

```
              ♠ 9 7
              ♡ 6 5
              ◇ K Q J 5 2
              ♣ K J 8 6
♠ A 6
♡ A K Q 8 4        ┌─────────┐
◇ A 9 3            │    N    │
♣ 9 7 3         W  │ W     E │  E
                   │    S    │
                   └─────────┘
```

| WEST | NORTH | EAST | SOUTH |
|------|-------|------|-------|
|      |       |      | 1♠ |
| 2♡ | dbl* | pass | 4♠ |
| all pass | | | |

You lead the ♡K and partner follows with the ♡2, a count signal that indicates three cards in the suit. How will you plan the defense?

# Problem 36

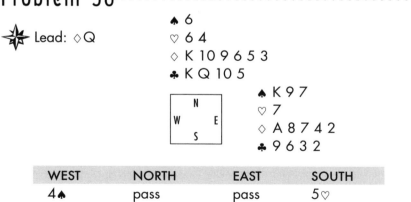 Lead: ◇Q

```
              ♠ 6
              ♡ 6 4
              ◇ K 10 9 6 5 3
              ♣ K Q 10 5
              ┌─────────┐      ♠ K 9 7
              │    N    │      ♡ 7
           W  │ W     E │  E   ◇ A 8 7 4 2
              │    S    │      ♣ 9 6 3 2
              └─────────┘
```

| WEST | NORTH | EAST | SOUTH |
|------|-------|------|-------|
| 4♠ | pass | pass | 5♡ |
| all pass | | | |

You are sitting East. What is your plan for the defense when partner leads the ◇Q and declarer plays low from the dummy?

```
                    ♠ K 4 3
                    ♡ A 6 2
                    ◇ A 8 7 5 2
                    ♣ 8 4
   ♠ 8 2                              ♠ 9 6
   ♡ J 10         ┌─────────┐         ♡ Q 9 7 4 3
   ◇ K Q J 9      │    N    │         ◇ 10 6
   ♣ A K Q J 3    │ W     E │         ♣ 9 7 6 2
                  │    S    │
                  └─────────┘
                    ♠ A Q J 10 7 5
                    ♡ K 8 5
                    ◇ 4 3
                    ♣ 10 5
```

| WEST | NORTH | EAST | SOUTH |
|------|-------|------|-------|
|      |       |      | 1♠ |
| 2♣ | 2◇ | pass | 2♠ |
| pass | 4♠ | all pass | |

*Sitting West, you lead the ♣K. The lead of a king requests a count signal (have you heard that somewhere before?) and partner follows with the ♣7, playing his second highest card from four. When you continue with the ♣A, partner plays the ♣2 and the ♣10 falls from declarer. Since South has considerably longer spades than East, it's odds on that he has only two clubs to East's four. This is backed up by the fact that East's chosen spot-cards conform to the second-then-fourth convention from four cards. How will you continue?*

Let's see what happened when the deal was actually played and West switched to an 'obvious' ◇K. Seeing that he would need to set up the diamonds, declarer cleverly ducked in the dummy. The contract could no longer be beaten. Whatever West did next, declarer would win and draw two rounds of trumps with the ace and queen. He would then cross to the ◇A and ruff a diamond. Returning to dummy with the ♠K, he would establish a long diamond with another ruff in the suit. Finally he would return to dummy with the ♡A to enjoy a discard on the long diamond.

To defeat the contract, West (you) must begin an attack on dummy's ♡A entry by switching to the ♡J. If declarer subsequently ducks a diamond, you can play another heart to remove the ♡A. With diamonds breaking 4-2, the contract can no longer be made.

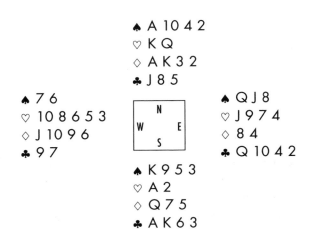

♠ A 10 4 2
♡ K Q
◇ A K 3 2
♣ J 8 5

♠ 7 6
♡ 10 8 6 5 3
◇ J 10 9 6
♣ 9 7

♠ Q J 8
♡ J 9 7 4
◇ 8 4
♣ Q 10 4 2

♠ K 9 5 3
♡ A 2
◇ Q 7 5
♣ A K 6 3

| WEST | NORTH | EAST | SOUTH |
|------|-------|------|-------|
|      |       |      | 1NT   |
| pass | 2♣    | pass | 2♠    |
| pass | 6♠    | all pass | |

*You are sitting East and your partner leads the ◇J against South's small slam in spades. Declarer wins with the ◇A in dummy and plays the ace and king of trumps, followed by the ace and king of hearts. He continues with the queen and king of diamonds. How will you defend?*

If you ruff the ◇K with your master trump, you will pay a heavy price. A club return will be allowed to run to dummy's ♣J and a third round of hearts will concede a ruff-and-sluff. Either way, declarer will lose no further trick. You should therefore discard a heart instead of ruffing. These cards will be left:

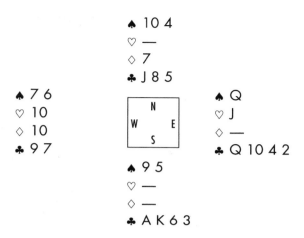

Suppose declarer now throws you in with a trump. What will you do?

If you exit with a club, declarer will make the slam. He will run your low club to dummy's jack and ruff the fourth round of clubs in dummy. Instead you must give a ruff-and-sluff. It will not help declarer to ruff in his hand and throw a club from dummy, because only one trump remains in dummy for ruffing clubs. Looking at it another way, declarer was bound to score his last two trumps separately anyway. What you must avoid is giving him three club tricks too.

Declarer's only other option (in the diagramed position) is to lead dummy's last diamond. If you throw the ♡J, declarer will ruff and throw you in with a trump to lead away from the ♣Q. You must therefore discard a club, retaining the ♡J as a safe exit card. Once again, the slam will be doomed.

```
                        ♠ 9 7
                        ♡ 6 5
                        ◇ K Q J 5 2
                        ♣ K J 8 6
    ♠ A 6                                  ♠ 4 2
    ♡ A K Q 8 4          ┌─────────┐       ♡ 9 3 2
    ◇ A 9 3           W  │    N    │  E    ◇ 10 8 7 6 4
    ♣ 9 7 3              │    S    │       ♣ 10 4 2
                        └─────────┘
                        ♠ K Q J 10 8 5 3
                        ♡ J 10 7
                        ◇ —
                        ♣ A Q 5
```

| WEST | NORTH | EAST | SOUTH |
|------|-------|------|-------|
|      |       |      | 1♠ |
| 2♡ | dbl* | pass | 4♠ |
| all pass | | | |

*Sitting West, you lead the ♡K against 4♠. Partner follows with the ♡2, a count signal that indicates three cards in the suit. (With five hearts he would surely have raised you.) How should you plan the defense?*

You expect to make two heart tricks and the ace of trumps is a banker for a third trick. Unless South has a diamond void, the contract will be down in top tricks. What can you do to cater for the case where South is void in the diamond suit?

It is no good playing ace and another trump, with the intention of preventing declarer from ruffing his third heart. If you follow that path declarer will score six trumps and four clubs for his game. The only defense to beat the contract is to switch to the ♠6 at Trick 2! Declarer has no counter to this. If he plays a second round of trumps, you will be able to cash two more heart winners. If instead declarer plays four rounds of clubs, seeking a heart discard, your partner will be able to ruff the fourth round of clubs with his remaining low trump.

What if declarer started with a singleton diamond and ♣A-Q? Your defense would allow him to discard his singleton diamond, yes, but the contract would still go down. Declarer would lose three hearts and one spade.

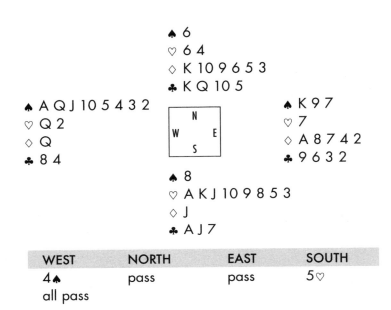

♠ 6
♡ 6 4
◇ K 10 9 6 5 3
♣ K Q 10 5

♠ A Q J 10 5 4 3 2
♡ Q 2
◇ Q
♣ 8 4

N
W   E
S

♠ K 9 7
♡ 7
◇ A 8 7 4 2
♣ 9 6 3 2

♠ 8
♡ A K J 10 9 8 5 3
◇ J
♣ A J 7

| WEST | NORTH | EAST | SOUTH |
|------|-------|------|-------|
| 4♠ | pass | pass | 5♡ |
| all pass | | | |

*Sitting East you decide to follow the maxim 'the five-level belongs to the opponents'. You pass out South's 5♡ bid and partner leads the ◇Q. What is your plan for the defense when declarer plays low from the dummy?*

Who holds the ◇J, would you say? Although ◇Q-J is a possible opening lead for West to choose, there are two reasons why you should be inclined to place South with the ◇J. The first is that South would probably have covered with dummy's ◇K if he had a diamond void. The second and stronger reason is that you are unlikely to defeat 5♡ if South is void in diamonds (South surely holds the ♣A, so where would your tricks come from?).

The best chance of defeating the contract is to score one spade trick, one diamond trick, and a trump trick promoted by returning a second round of diamonds. How can you achieve this aim? Should you play the ◇8 at Trick 1, hoping that partner reads this as a suit-preference signal for a spade switch to your king? That's what some players would do, but there is no need to put your partner under such strain. Instead you should overtake the ◇Q with the ◇A. Now what?

If you return a second round of diamonds immediately, the contract will survive. Declarer will discard his singleton spade. Your partner's ♡Q will be promoted, yes, but you will no longer be able to score a spade trick. To prevent this happening, you must cash the ♠K at Trick 2. Only then do you return a second diamond. Declarer has no escape. Whether he ruffs with the ace or the jack, he will go down one.

Suppose the holdings had been somewhat different and you had seen this position from the East seat:

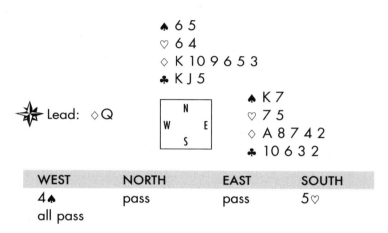

♠ 6 5
♡ 6 4
◇ K 10 9 6 5 3
♣ K J 5

Lead: ◇Q

♠ K 7
♡ 7 5
◇ A 8 7 4 2
♣ 10 6 3 2

| WEST | NORTH | EAST | SOUTH |
| --- | --- | --- | --- |
| 4♠ | pass | pass | 5♡ |
| all pass | | | |

Again West leads the ◇Q, not covered, and you overtake with the ◇A. Now there are two chances to beat the contract. The trump promotion we have just seen might be available. Alternatively, if partner holds only seven spades, you might be able to score two spade tricks. Which is it to be?

There is no need to guess if you play count signals! You lead the ♠K at Trick 2. If partner plays high, indicating an even number of spades (eight, here), you will know that a second spade trick is not available and will try your luck with a second round of diamonds. If instead partner gives you a low count signal, you will play a spade at Trick 3. In this way you beat the contract in either situation.